We Make Mistakes, Mistakes Make Us

Stop making something out of nothing and start making something out of nothing.

Tarek Riman

Copyright © 2024 Tarek Riman

All rights reserved.

ISBN: 9798335007290

DEDICATION

To God, Allah, Jesus, Universe.

To Biscotti, Alex and Melissa.

To my Family Toufic, Tameem, Ghazi, Hala.

To my close friends who believed in me.

To the beautiful souls that I met along the way.

For the angels in my life.

To you, Coco, RIP my beautiful dog. I love you.

To you.

I love you.

We make mistakes, Mistakes make us.

Registration No. 1217259
Canadian Intellectual Property Office | An Agency of Industry Canada
© Copyright 2024 by Tarek Riman
All Rights Reserved.
No part of this book may be reproduced in any form or by any means
(electronic or mechanical, including photocopying, recording or by an
information storage and retrieval system), without written permission from
the author, except for the inclusion of brief excerpts for review purposes or
personal use by the purchaser, and referenced as per appropriate methods.
Permission should be addressed in writing to triman@captaim.com.

DISCLAIMER

This book is designed to provide information, motivation and empowerment
to readers. It is sold with the understanding that the author is not assured to
deliver any kind of psychological advice (e.g. legal, medical, psychological) or
be a substitute for professional assistance. No warranties or guarantees are
expressed or implied by the writer in the content of this volume. The author
shall not be liable for any physical, psychological, emotional, financial or
commercial damages, including, but not limited to, special, incidental,
consequential or other damages. The reader is responsible for their own
choices, actions, and results. Situations, people and context have been
changed as appropriate to protect the privacy of others.

Cover Wrap by Nancy Morris

First Printing, 2024
ISBN: 9798335007290

ACKNOWLEDGMENTS

"This book is a powerful reminder that mistakes are not failures, but opportunities for growth. The author masterfully weaves personal stories with profound insights, showing us that our greatest strengths often emerge from our most challenging moments. A must-read for anyone on a journey of self-discovery and personal growth."

**Melissa Dawn, Founder CEO of Your Life
Montreal, Quebec, Canada**

"An inspiring and thought-provoking read, this book challenges the notion that talent alone leads to success. Through compelling narratives and practical advice, the author demonstrates that grit, resilience, and the willingness to embrace mistakes are the true drivers of lasting achievement. A brilliant guide to cultivating a growth mindset and living life to its fullest."

Marcos Carvalho, Co-Founder

Introduction

Over the course of my life, I've navigated the complexities of war, explored distant lands, and absorbed countless lessons along the way. I've had the privilege of teaching tens of thousands of students, dedicating tens of thousands of hours to my work and personal growth. My journey has taken me on eight pilgrimages, most notably along the Camino de Santiago in Europe, where I've sought not only physical endurance but also spiritual enlightenment.

My experiences have been diverse and transformative, from practicing martial arts to embracing the disciplines of meditation and breathing exercises. But perhaps most importantly, I've made hundreds of mistakes—each one a stepping stone that has shaped who I am today. The wisdom I've gained from these experiences, along with the invaluable lessons passed down from my mentors, has been the cornerstone of my personal and professional growth.

In this book, I will share with you the lessons I've learned, the mistakes I've made, and the unique perspectives and approaches that have guided me. My hope is that by sharing these insights, you too will find value in them, and that they will help you navigate your own path with greater clarity and purpose.

Table of Contents

" Poem 16

Impermanence – By Tarek Riman 16

Chapter 1.1 19

A bit of perspective – An angle on life. 19

Chapter 1.2 21

The World You Know Will Disappear in a Few Hundred Years 21

" Poem 28

Happiness – By Tarek Riman 28

Chapter 2.1 31

The Essence of Happiness 31

Chapter 2.2 35

The Choice You Enjoy 35

Chapter 2.3 38

Negative Emotion Avoidance Doesn't Mean Happiness 38

Chapter 2.4 41

Happiness Is Not About Work or Money; It Is About Being Kinder to Yourself 41

Chapter 2.5 45

The Happy Eyes You Are Looking Through into the World Are Yours. The Angry Eyes as Well 45

Chapter 2.6 53

Worrying and Forgetting - What Are You So Worried About? 53

" Poem 59

"With gratitude as your compass, and trust as your guide." – by Tarek Riman 59

Chapter 3.1 62

Trust the Process, My Friend, Trust the Process.................62

Chapter 3.2 69

Something Has Been Given to You: Life....................69

Chapter 3.3 72

The Sun Will Always Shine 72

Chapter 3.4 75

Look at the Gift in Everything.........................75

" Poem....................................84

"Compass Within." – by Tarek Riman....................84

Chapter 4.1 87

Know What Is Good and Right.........................87

Chapter 4.2 92

Accept Triumph and Disaster.........................92

Research Late at Night, Make Decisions in the Morning 99

Chapter 4.4 105

Worn out tools..................................105

Chapter 4.5 110

Ask, and You Will Only Ask a Stupid Question Once 110

Chapter 4.6 116

Learn and Avoid Going to the School of Hard Knocks.......116

Chapter 4.7 124

Always Get a Rough First Draft, Don't Wait Too Long.......124

Chapter 4.8 127

Don't Be Afraid to Risk It All and Start Over Again.........127

Chapter 4.9 132

People & the World: Either Teach and Create – Don't Complain 132

Chapter 4.10 135

Listen to People You Don't Get Along With 135

Chapter 4.11 142

All You Had to Do Is Ask and Aim 142

" Poem 149

"Lives Within." – by Tarek Riman 149

Chapter 5.1 151

You Don't Have to Win Everything 151

Chapter 5.2 158

Treat Yourself Like You Would Treat a Loved One - Who Are You Putting on a Pedestal? 158

Chapter 5.3 162

How You Treat Yourself 162

Chapter 5.4 165

What Is Good for You Is Better Than What You Want 165

Chapter 5.5 171

Stop Trying to Prove Yourself 171

Chapter 5.6 175

Talent Alone 175

Chapter 5.7 182

Find Meaning 182

Chapter 5.8 186

What Bothers You Now Won't Bother You in the Future 186

Chapter 5.9 189

If You Are 35 Now and Cynical and Angry, in 10 Years, It Will Be 10 Times Worse 189

Chapter 5.10 193

We Make Mistakes, Mistakes Make Us

You Have to Change Your Ways, or You Will Go Down a Dreadful Path 193

" Poem 197

"Me and you" – by Tarek Riman 197

Chapter 6.1 200

People are good. 200

Chapter 6.2 205

Helping each other 205

Chapter 6.3 213

Understand Family 213

" Poem 218

"I clipped my wings"– by Tarek Riman 218

Chapter 7.1 221

Fail to Protect Yourself, and You Will Set Yourself Free - Protection Is the Enemy of Freedom 221

Chapter 7.2 226

We Build Golden Castles to Live In, They Become Our Prison 226

Chapter 7.3 231

Minimalism - Less Is More 231

" Poem 240

"Mistakes we make"– by Tarek Riman 240

Chapter 8.1 243

Mistakes Have Nothing to Do with Your Character 243

Chapter 8.2 248

We Make Mistakes, and Mistakes Make Us 248

I will leave you with this 254

"Life unbound" – by Tarek Riman 254

About the Author.. 255

We Make Mistakes, Mistakes Make Us

" Poem

Impermanence – By Tarek Riman

Life is a shifting tapestry, woven with threads of change,
A journey through uncertainty, where nothing stays the same.
We chase control, seek permanence, in a world that never stills,
But the essence of our happiness lies in how we face these hills.

You find yourself in a moment, caught in trivial cares,
Overwhelmed by daily stresses, by life's relentless snares.
But step back and gain perspective, see the broader view,
The world will keep on turning, and so, my friend, will you.

In ancient towns with cobblestone streets, I've wandered,
Through places rich with history, where countless lives have pondered.
The walls, the roads, the borders—all will fade away,
But what remains eternal is how we live today.

We build our lives on shifting sands, in search of something more,
Yet true peace comes from knowing that change is at our core.
The castles we admire will crumble into dust,
The cities we inhabit will give way to time's slow rust.

But rather than despair, find solace in this truth,
That life's impermanence is what gives it depth and youth.
Embrace the fleeting moments, for they are all we have,
And let go of the burdens that make your heart feel sad.

The world you know will vanish, like a dream at break of day,
But the love, the joy, the kindness—you leave those as your stay.
So live not in the future, nor be haunted by the past,
Trust in the journey's process, and let each moment last.

We Make Mistakes, Mistakes Make Us

When the worries of tomorrow weigh heavy on your mind,
Remember that in letting go, true freedom you will find.
For in the grand expanse of time, our worries are but small,
And what matters most is how we choose to rise, each time we fall.

Perspective is a gift, a lens through which to see,
That life is full of wonder, of possibility.
So do not cling too tightly to the things you cannot hold,
But embrace the beauty of the now, let your story unfold.

Chapter 1
Perspective

Summary: Life is a complex, ever-changing journey that defies simple definitions of right and wrong, good and bad. As we navigate through its twists and turns, we often find ourselves caught in the pursuit of control, stability, and certainty. Yet, the irony lies in our desire for permanence in a constantly shifting world. In this chapter, we explore the idea that life is not about rigidly clinging to what we know but rather about embracing the unpredictability of the journey. Whether you place your faith in God, the Universe, or the simple flow of existence, the key to a fulfilling life lies in letting go, trusting the process, and finding peace in the midst of life's inherent uncertainties. Here, we begin a journey of reflection, where the essence of life is not in its predictability but in its surprises and the growth they inspire.

My Mistake is that I allow myself to get stuck in and overwhelmed by trivial matters, whether they involve work, life, education, or a big classroom. In this chapter, I will share how I put things into perspective to help address this better.

Chapter 1.1

A bit of perspective – An angle on life.

There is no right or wrong, good or bad. Life is what it is. You move through it, learn from it, and grow. The irony lies in our human nature; we seek steadiness in a constantly changing world. We strive for control when, in reality, we need to let go. We worry about where life will lead us, fearing our past mistakes, when we should instead trust the journey—whether it be guided by God, the Universe, Allah, or Jesus. As children, we love surprises; as adults, we avoid them. We forget how just to be, so we keep ourselves busy. We lose the ability to do nothing, even though sometimes, doing nothing is precisely what we need.

Life itself is a pilgrimage, filled with suffering along the way. But that's not necessarily bad; it's simply the reality of our limited time here. Knowing this, you owe it to yourself to travel, live through this pilgrimage with acceptance, and be unafraid of getting hurt. Trust that whatever happens is just a part of the journey, an unavoidable part. Remember, you are on a rock travelling through space with just the right amount of oxygen, atmosphere, and sunlight—you are already the luckiest creature in the universe. So don't take anything too seriously, especially not the things others tell you to take seriously, or even yourself. I've seen more abandoned houses full of memories and broken dreams than I can count, and I've made more mistakes than most people my age. So, trust me when I say nothing lasts. Time is the most consistent thing in the world, and the key to making the most of it is counterintuitive: ignore it and give it the most minor importance possible.

Chapter 1.2

The World You Know Will Disappear in a Few Hundred Years

A few years ago, I embarked on a journey I had dreamed of for as long as I could remember. I set out to visit every European country, determined to experience the rich tapestry of history, culture, and life the continent had to offer. I didn't just want to see the sights; I wanted to feel the pulse of each place, walk its streets, meet its people, and immerse myself in the stories that had shaped it.

I travelled by bike through most of these countries, taking the long roads that wound through villages, forests, and mountains. I walked through ancient towns, their cobblestone streets echoing with the footsteps of generations long gone. I stood in awe before grand cathedrals that had witnessed centuries of history and crossed borders redrawn countless times by the tides of war and peace.

As I journeyed from one country to the next, a realization began to take root in my mind: everything I was seeing—every stone, every building, every border—was part of a world that, in a few hundred years, would no longer exist as I knew it. The grand castles would crumble, the bustling cities would transform, and the vibrant cultures would evolve into something new. The world I was experiencing was but a fleeting moment in the vast timeline of human history.

At first, this thought was unsettling. It's human nature to seek permanence and comfort in the idea that the things we know and love will endure. But as I continued my travels, this perspective began to shift. I started to see the world's impermanence not as something to fear but as something profoundly liberating.

One day, as I biked through the sun-soaked hills of Spain, I came upon a small village nestled between rolling vineyards and olive groves. With its terracotta rooftops and narrow streets, the town looked like it had been frozen in time. The stone houses were adorned with colourful flower boxes, and the air was filled with the scent of jasmine. I decided to stop and explore, letting my bike rest against an ancient stone wall.

As I wandered through the village, I was drawn to the central plaza, where a centuries-old fountain trickled quietly in the afternoon sun. I sat on a worn wooden bench in the square, taking in the peaceful scene. The villagers went about their day, their lives seemingly untouched by the rush of the modern world. It was easy to imagine that little had changed here over the past few hundred years.

Sitting there, I was struck by how many people had passed through this village over the centuries, each with their own stories, worries, and dreams. Where were they now? What had become of their world? In a few hundred years, what would become of this village, this moment, this world that I was now a part of?

Instead of feeling a sense of loss, I felt a profound sense of peace. The world's impermanence didn't seem frightening—it felt like a gentle reminder of the beauty of life's fleeting nature. The world changes, people come and go, and yet life continues, always evolving, always renewing itself.

This perspective changed the way I saw my own life. The worries that had once consumed me—about my career, future, and place in the world—began to feel lighter, less burdensome. I understood that just as the world around me was transient, so too were my challenges and fears. They were just moments in time, part of a journey that would continue to unfold in ways I couldn't predict.

As I continued my travels, I carried this newfound understanding with me. I became more present, more focused on the here and now, rather than getting caught up in concerns about the future. I met people whose lives were vastly different from mine, each with their own stories and struggles, and I realized that we were all part of the same ever-changing world. What mattered was not holding on to the past or worrying about the future but embracing the present and finding meaning in our lives.

When I finally completed my journey and returned home, I brought memories of the places I had visited and a more profound sense of acceptance and peace. The world I knew—the world we all know—would one day disappear, replaced by something new. And that was okay. It was all part of the natural flow of life.

Whenever I find myself overwhelmed by the moment's challenges, I remember that village in Spain, the bench in the square, and the realization that everything is temporary. It reminds me to focus on what truly matters—to live fully, love deeply, and appreciate each fleeting moment's beauty.

The world we know will disappear in a few hundred years, but the impact of how we choose to live our lives today will resonate far beyond our time. And that is a legacy worth embracing.

We Make Mistakes, Mistakes Make Us

" Poem

Happiness – By Tarek Riman

Happiness isn't a destination far or grand,
But crafted in choices made by your own hand.
It's not the wealth you amass or the things you own,
But the gratitude you show for seeds you've sown.

You arrive in a city, with pockets not full,
Yet content in your heart, free from worry's pull.
Friends complain of the finest, still craving for more,
While you find joy in small gifts, in life's simple store.

True happiness isn't found in avoiding the rain,
But in embracing the storms, and growing through pain.
It's knowing the light after darkness is sweet,
And understanding that both joy and sorrow must meet.

You make a choice, and wonder if it's right,
But happiness comes not from the choice, but the light—
You bring to each moment, the love you allow,
To flourish within, here and now.

Happiness is not avoiding what's tough,
But being kind to yourself when life is rough.
It's the lens through which you view your days,
Choosing to see blessings, and the world in new ways.

So, don't be fooled by what others say,
Happiness is shaped by you, in your own unique way.
It's the quiet contentment in knowing you're enough,
And finding peace, even when the journey is tough.

We Make Mistakes, Mistakes Make Us

Worry less about the future's unknown,
For happiness is in the moments you own.
It's the choice to be present, to embrace where you stand,
And to live each day fully, by your own hand.

Chapter 2
Happiness

Summary: Happiness, often seen as a distant goal, is in reality shaped by the small choices we make every day. It's not a grand destination but a journey built on gratitude, self-awareness, and the way we choose to perceive our experiences. In a world where we are constantly bombarded with messages that more is better, we easily forget that true happiness comes from within, not from external circumstances. This chapter delves into the power of gratitude as the foundation of contentment, the importance of making choices that align with our values, and the realization that happiness isn't about avoiding negative emotions but understanding and embracing them. It's a reminder that the way we look at the world, the way we treat ourselves, and the choices we make each day ultimately shape our experience of happiness.

My mistake: No one teaches you how to be happy, and they shouldn't because what makes us happy is different from what makes others happy. This chapter looks at the essence of being happy and joyful.

Chapter 2.1

The Essence of Happiness

Gratitude turns what you have into enough if not more than enough.

Let me tell you a story.

I arrived in London to see friends who were supposed to meet me there, and as always, when travelling, I travelled light and with minimal cost. I aimed to live within my means and travel within my limits. Nonetheless, I always made time for my travels. I never felt the need to show off. I always believed that what I had was just enough.

As I got to see my friends staying in one of the best hotels in London, I stepped into this perfect hotel right across from Hyde Park in the middle of the city. The stone entrance, the carpet, the lights, the piano, the fine gentleman who opened the door—it was all beautiful and perfect. While waiting for my friends, I noticed there were free apples. I grabbed a few, put them in my bag, and ate one. I smelled it beforehand and felt so grateful for just being in that hallway.

Especially me, a budget traveller. I often asked friends to host me and wouldn't mind sleeping on a couch—not for lack of money, but because I preferred to spend on experiences rather than accommodation, especially when travelling alone. After a 30-minute wait, my friends arrived from their room, and the first thing they did was complain about the hotel. They said it wasn't ideal, the gifts weren't good, and it was too much. I was shocked because, to be honest, everything seemed perfect. But who was I to judge? This hit close to home because I had been down that path before where I had everything yet had nothing.

Throughout the evening, I kept listening to my friends as they complained. They even complained that the new Mercedes Benz EQS, the car of my dreams that picked them up from the airport, wasn't good enough. All of this was beyond my wildest dreams, beyond what I could sustainably afford in the long term. Not to mention, the company paid for it. It was free, yet they still weren't happy. Meanwhile, I was flying on a budget, using public transport, and walking everywhere, and I was just fine. I wasn't jumping with joy, but I was grateful.

If the world isn't enough, how can we be enough? If the best of the best isn't good enough, maybe money isn't the answer. Don't get me wrong, I've been poor a few times, and I don't want to go back. But I think, past a certain threshold, money can't change anything. Gratitude is key; it humbles with its perspective. It makes you understand that what you've been given is borrowed, and it's not yours. Even your time, body, and mind are not yours. You will soon stop existing, and all that you complained about won't matter. Gratitude is the gift of the present. It's the well that keeps giving. Without it, we are lost between complaints and disappointment.

Chapter 2.2

The Choice You Enjoy

Happiness is not a destination; it's a series of choices we make every day. It's crucial to choose activities, careers, and relationships that bring joy and fulfillment. When you align your life with your passions and values, the path to happiness becomes clearer and more attainable. Enjoying the choices you make leads to a more content and satisfied life.

A few months ago, my friend David called me. He had just bought an FJ Cruiser. He was delighted with the car for the first few days, but then he called me again and said, "I'm not sure about this. I'm having severe buyer's remorse. I'm not sure I'll be able to enjoy this decision that I've made. Maybe I shouldn't have sold that Wrangler. Maybe I should have kept it; it was much cheaper than the new car."

I replied, "The choice you enjoy will always be right."

Even if you think you made the wrong choice, it's not bad unless you suffer, and most suffering is self-inflicted. It doesn't matter what decision you made—whether right or wrong—because honestly, it doesn't make a difference. It's all a matter of time, space, and the state of the world. What might be wrong today could be right in 20 years. Look how much the world has changed recently. In just one decade, everything has changed. What is acceptable now was never acceptable when I was a kid. What is acceptable where I live in Canada was never acceptable when I lived in Lebanon.

So, your decision—whether right or wrong—doesn't matter. What matters is how you handle it and what you do about it. I'm not here to motivate or demotivate you about your decision. I'm trying to say that whatever decision you make, choose to enjoy it. Choose to enjoy the ride. Yes, you've taken the wrong turn. Yes, you might have bought something beyond your means. If you do, you'll lose twice if you don't enjoy it. At least appreciate that you purchased something beyond your means, and then it's worth it. Then it's going to be worth every single penny that you spend.

It was easy for me to say that because, by that time, I had been in Europe for around three and a half weeks. I was far away from home, living a life of adventure and travel. I had already visited six new countries on that trip. I was so happy with myself, telling myself along the way, "I'm so far away from my office. I'm so far away from my clients. I'm so far away from my university. It's a bit uncomfortable, but all this discomfort would have gone to waste. All this discomfort would have gone to waste if I did not enjoy my trip and make the best out of it."

Chapter 2.3

Negative Emotion Avoidance Doesn't Mean Happiness

Avoiding negative emotions is not the same as being happy. True happiness comes from acknowledging and processing your positive and negative emotions. Suppressing sadness, anger, or fear can lead to more significant distress over time. Instead, allow yourself to feel and understand these emotions, using them as a guide to make necessary changes and find balance in your life.

I was hiking the Swiss Alps with one of my close friends, Tom. After a few hours of hiking, we stopped at a coffee shop. The coffee shop had some of the best coffee I've ever tried. It was in the middle of Lausanne, Switzerland. The coffee was exceptional. I always order Americano, but before I placed my order, Tom looked at me and said, "Trust me, order the cappuccino." So cappuccino it was. We went outside and sat with nice views of the Swiss Alps right in front of us.

Tom looked at me and said, "Do you see how good this feels? Do you know what this is? This is happiness." And he added, "Happiness is the absence of suffering."

Tom is my friend, and I agree with much of what he says, but I don't agree with ending the sentence there. I would change it from "happiness is the absence of suffering" to "happiness is the absence of suffering after you've experienced suffering." If you've never experienced suffering, you'll never understand happiness. We're not happy because we're not suffering. We are happy despite suffering. We need to understand, feel, and fully accept the ups and downs of life to experience happiness.

The way I see it, I found the most happiness when I was doing a few things: when I was productive and had a good sense of accomplishment and achievement in my life, when I was grateful, at peace, and in complete trust of the current moment that I was in, and when I was fully engaged in something meaningful, such as reading or writing, or teaching at a university. A sense of meaning always brought me the most happiness possible. And lastly, when I was in love, even though love is never easy—even in heartbreak, heartache, and the complete surrender to the beauty of love—I was feeling an emotion that I would like to call happiness.

I'm in no position to give any advice on happiness. I was born into a tough country, raised in a strict household, and have endured some challenging moments here and there. Happiness did not come easy in my life. I could write a book on suffering but leave it at one chapter regarding joy.

Chapter 2.4

Happiness Is Not About Work or Money; It Is About Being Kinder to Yourself

While work and financial stability are essential, they are not the ultimate sources of happiness. Being kind to yourself, practicing self-care, and nurturing your mental and emotional well-being are far more critical. Happiness comes from self-compassion and treating yourself with the same kindness and understanding you would offer to a friend.

Growing up with an immigrant mentality isn't necessarily wrong or right—it's just a way of life. Nonetheless, it teaches you how to be hard on yourself. If I were to tell some of my relatives right now that they need to be kinder to themselves, they would laugh and say, "Is that something you've learned in Canada? Are you Canadian now? Have you been Canadianized?"

Instead of taking any insult from this conversation, I look back at them and ask a straightforward question: What has being hard on yourself ever brought you?

Most of the time, they don't even know how to answer. I do get the occasional response, like, "Boy, we were hard on you, and your parents were hard on you, and look where you ended up. Not bad."

To that, I answer, "I ended up where I am exactly because I was kind to myself. Because I owe it to myself to be kind to myself."

Here's the truth: There is a clear correlation between how willing you are to fail and being kind to yourself. The harder you are on yourself, the less willing you are to fail. And the less willing you are to fail, the less your chances of succeeding.

As I get older, I realize that the harder I am on myself, the harder other people will be on me because that permits them to treat me the same way I treat myself. If I treat myself with love and respect in front of others, then they wouldn't dare treat me otherwise.

I can't count the number of times I've heard people tell me, "Tarek, why is everybody so hard on me? Why can't I catch a break?"

My answer is always the same: When you start treating yourself properly, others will start treating you the same. You cannot demand something from others you haven't earned from yourself, and you can't ask someone to love you if you haven't chosen to love yourself first.

Love yourself.

And here's the vicious cycle: Initially, I didn't know how to love myself, especially after all the failures I had been through. The only way I could get any affirmation was through being productive, also known as making money. And guess what? I became the most productive person I've ever met. I started working 120 hours per week. I put my blood, sweat, and tears into my business, which grew. But after growing my business and being exceptionally productive, I can tell you one thing—none of this brought me happiness. It might have brought me an initial rush, but it never brought me joy. The only time I was able to achieve true happiness was by giving myself enough time to reflect on everything I'd done and when I started telling myself that I'd done okay for myself.

On the way up, I received a lot of compliments, but none of them meant anything to me. The only compliment that truly mattered was the one that came from me. It wasn't until I was fully burned out, overworked, down, and on an extremely rough path that I realized no one owes you your happiness; you owe it to yourself.

Chapter 2.5

The Happy Eyes You Are Looking Through into the World Are Yours. The Angry Eyes as Well

Life often feels like a constant tug-of-war between the good and the bad, the joyful and the painful. We all navigate through a world that presents us with challenges and triumphs, setbacks and successes. Yet, how we experience these moments—how we feel about them, interpret them, and ultimately, how they shape us—is deeply influenced by the lens through which we choose to see the world.

It's easy to blame our circumstances for the way we feel. When things go wrong, when stress mounts and frustrations boil over, it's natural to think that the world is against us, that our unhappiness is a direct result of external forces. But what if the truth is more complex than that? What if the way we see the world has more to do with our internal state than with anything happening around us?

In this chapter, we'll explore the powerful truth that the eyes we choose to look through—whether happy, angry, or anything in between—are our own. The world reflects back on what we project onto it, and by shifting our perspective, we have the power to transform not just how we see the world but also how we experience it. It's a lesson that's easy to overlook in the rush of daily life but one that can profoundly change the way we live.

Let's dive in and see how our friends—people like Helen, Tom, and Lucy—have grappled with this truth, and how it has reshaped their lives, just as it can reshape yours.

Take Helen, for instance. We've been friends since

college, and I've always admired her resilience. She's a single mother of two, working two jobs just to keep things afloat. Every day, she's up before dawn, juggling her kids' schedules, her work responsibilities, and the endless tasks that come with running a household. When we talk, she's often exhausted, worn down by the relentless grind. She rarely complains, but I can see the toll it's taking on her. The love she has for her children is evident, but the weight of her responsibilities is starting to obscure that love, turning her daily life into a series of stressful obligations rather than moments of joy.

Then there's Tom, my friend from the early days of our careers. Tom's always been the ambitious type— climbing the corporate ladder with determination. But with each promotion, he's found himself more isolated. His days are filled with back-to-back meetings, endless emails, and the pressure to deliver results. When we catch up, I see a man who's constantly on edge, battling a never-ending tide of responsibilities. He's achieved so much, yet he's struggling to find satisfaction in his success. The career he once loved now feels like a burden, and he's started questioning whether all the sacrifices have been worth it.

And then there's Lucy. She's the youngest in our group, full of potential and drive, but lately, she's been plagued by doubt. Social media has become her measuring stick, and no matter what she achieves, it never seems to measure up to the curated lives she sees online. Every time we talk, I hear the frustration in her voice—the feeling that she's constantly chasing an impossible standard. She's brilliant and capable, yet she's trapped in a cycle of comparison that's slowly draining her of the confidence she once had.

These are my friends—people I care about deeply—and it hurts to see them struggle. But as I've watched them, I've come to realize something important: the way we experience life is largely determined by the perspective we choose to adopt.

Life is undeniably tough. Helen's challenges as a

single mother, Tom's isolation at the top of his career, Lucy's battle with self-worth—these are not trivial problems. They're real, and they're hard. But the harsh truth is that while we can't always control the situations we find ourselves in, we can control how we respond to them.

This realization hit me one evening after a particularly grueling day at work. I was exhausted, mentally and physically drained, and on the verge of letting all the stress get the best of me. But as I sat there, reflecting on the day, I thought about my friends and what they were going through. I realized that we were all caught up in this endless cycle of stress and dissatisfaction, not because our lives were inherently miserable, but because we were allowing ourselves to see them that way.

It was then that I decided to change the narrative— not just for myself, but for all of us.

I reached out to Helen first. I didn't give her a pep

talk or offer superficial advice. Instead, I asked her to describe one moment from her day that brought her genuine joy, no matter how small. She paused, then told me about a quiet moment she had shared with her daughter that morning, just before the chaos of the day began. It was a fleeting moment, but it was beautiful. I encouraged her to hold onto that, to let that be the lens through which she viewed her day. It wasn't about ignoring the hard parts—it was about acknowledging the good ones and letting them matter just as much.

Next, I met with Tom over a beer. We talked about work, as we often did, but I pushed the conversation further. I asked him what he missed most about his early days in the career he used to love. He admitted that he missed the camaraderie, the feeling of being part of a team. Somewhere along the way, the climb had turned into a solitary pursuit. I suggested that he find ways to reconnect with that sense of teamwork, whether by mentoring younger colleagues or simply making more time for meaningful interactions at work. It wasn't a solution to all his problems, but it was a step toward finding purpose again.

And then there was Lucy. We went for a walk one evening, and I listened as she vented about her frustrations and insecurities. When she was done, I didn't try to convince her that she was wrong to feel that way. Instead, I challenged her to define success on her own terms, rather than letting social media dictate it. I asked her to focus on the progress she had made, to set goals that were meaningful to her, and to celebrate her own achievements, no matter how small they seemed in comparison to others. It wasn't about dismissing her feelings—it was about helping her see her worth through a different lens.

As I watched my friends start to shift their perspectives, I realized that this was the real work of life—not just achieving goals or overcoming obstacles, but learning to see the world in a way that allows us to find meaning and joy, even in the midst of struggle. It's about choosing which eyes we look through—the ones clouded by stress, frustration, and dissatisfaction, or the ones that can see beauty, purpose, and possibility.

The truth is, life is always going to be a mix of good and bad, joy and pain, success and failure. We can't change that. But we can change how we choose to see it. And in that choice lies our power.

Helen still has her hard days, but she's learned to find those moments of joy and let them sustain her. Tom is rediscovering what he loves about his work, focusing on the connections he's making rather than just the climb. And Lucy is starting to see herself not through the distorted lens of social media, but through the reality of her own accomplishments and potential.

We're all still figuring it out, but I think we're on the right track. We've learned that the eyes we look through shape our experience of the world. And by choosing to see through eyes of gratitude, purpose, and self-compassion, we're finding our way to a life that feels richer, more fulfilling, and ultimately, more real.

Chapter 2.6

Worrying and Forgetting - What Are You So Worried About?

My grandpa used to say, "A tough day is coming; it's going to come no matter what—whether you like it or not, whether you do everything right or not, whether you do everything by the book or not. A tough day is coming." A tough day is coming, whether you worry about it or not. If you worry about that harrowing day, you will just ruin today and every day in between.

My grandpa's answer to tough days was simple: "There's no point in worrying," he said. "I lived around 80 years on this planet and worried about a lot of things. My only regret is that I worried about them." No matter how much we worry, we have no control over most of our lives, other people's lives, or the future.

I had my own encounters with worrying throughout my life. Coming from a country like Lebanon, you cannot live without a bit of worry—or you might literally die. As I progressed in my career and travelled the world, I worried more than I should have. It wasn't until I was on one of my pilgrimages in Extremadura, in the south of Spain, that I genuinely confronted my worries. I was on a pilgrimage called Camino de Santiago, specifically Camino de La Plata, which goes from Seville to Santiago in Galicia.

This is one of the less popular Camino routes. In the north, on the Camino Frances, you might run into hundreds of people every hour during the high season. But on this route, even in late May, I met very few people. Those I did meet were strong, fit, and seemed to be there not for tourism but for the suffering or the chosen loneliness.

As I walked through the hills north of Seville, nearing

the city of Merida, there was an eerie sense of familiarity. Ninety percent of what I saw felt like something I had already seen. I was in a rush—a rush I created for myself, one that was never imposed upon me. I felt I needed to be 100 kilometres ahead of where I was at that moment. Not the right attitude to have on a pilgrimage, I tell you.

When you're in a hurry, you lose the sense of being present. A small rock in your path becomes an obstacle instead of a beautiful artifact of nature. A delicious tortilla with café con leche becomes a necessity for regaining energy rather than a delightful Spanish meal in a quaint village.

This perspective didn't change until I met an old man, a French gentleman from Toulon. I wasn't in the mood for conversation, but when he greeted me with "Bonjour," I replied with "Bonjour, comment ça va?" We started chatting, exchanging the usual questions about where we were from and why we were there.

After an hour of conversation, I said I had to go. I needed to be in a certain town by a certain time. He asked, "Or what?" He repeated my words: "You need to be in this town by this time, or what?" I answered, "I don't know."

He laughed, looked me in the eye, and asked me to sit down in the middle of the road. "What are you so worried about? Where do you want to be?" I didn't know. He told me, "I was you. I lived all my life worrying, wanting to be somewhere else. Now, as I'm older, the only place I want to be is right here."

He asked me to close my eyes and imagine being wherever I wanted to be and how I would feel if I were there. I closed my eyes and did as he said. I felt nothing different. I realized I felt the same way as I did at that moment, always needing to be somewhere else.

He told me, "You're either here or nowhere. You can't be in two places at once. This is it, my friend. There's nowhere else in the world but here."

We get preoccupied with where we want to be, we forget how to enjoy life.

Worrying often stems from fear of the unknown or concern about potential negative outcomes. It's important to question the source of your worries and evaluate their validity. Many worries are based on hypothetical scenarios that may never materialize. By identifying and addressing the root causes of your worries, you can reduce their impact on your mental well-being.

We Make Mistakes, Mistakes Make Us

" Poem

"With gratitude as your compass, and trust as your guide." – by Tarek Riman

In the journey of life, trust is key,
Without it, you suffer and struggle to see.
Trust in yourself, in the process at hand,
For it's in trusting, that you truly understand.

You step out in faith, on paths unknown,
Leaving behind the comfort of home.
On the Camino de Santiago, I've walked time and again,
And each time I'm reminded, of the beauty in the strain.

Through foreign lands and unfamiliar ways,
I've found that trust is what truly pays.
In every struggle, an angel appears,
A kind soul to calm my fears.

But it's not just on distant roads I find,
These angels walk with me, every time.
In Canada's streets or Spain's rough terrain,
Trust in life, and you'll find there's much to gain.

Yet how often we forget, what's been given to us,
We worry and fret, make life such a fuss.
But life itself is the greatest gift of all,
And when we see it as such, our burdens feel small.

We Make Mistakes, Mistakes Make Us

We aren't owed success, nor happiness on demand,
But the sun will always rise, as planned.
Even in the darkest night, when all hope seems lost,
Remember, the light will come, no matter the cost.

I've faced loss, deep and true,
And through it all, I knew—
That the sun would shine again, bright and clear,
Bringing with it, a new day, a chance to steer.

The road was rough, the path unclear,
But through each trial, something dear.
Lessons learned in the hardest of times,
Are the ones that echo, like chimes.

So look for the gifts in life's twists and turns,
In every struggle, there's something to learn.
Trust the process, embrace each day,
With gratitude in your heart, you'll find your way.

For life is fleeting, a precious loan,
A journey through which we're never alone.
The world will change, the sun will set,
But the impact we make—we'll never forget.

Live fully, love deeply, and trust in the ride,
With gratitude as your compass, and trust as your guide.
There's a gift in everything, if only we see,
Life's true treasures are in the moments we're free.

Chapter 3
Gratitude

Summary

Life is an unpredictable journey filled with challenges, moments of joy, and opportunities for growth. In the following chapters, I share personal stories and reflections that highlight the importance of trust, gratitude, resilience, and perspective. Through these narratives, I invite you to explore the deeper meanings behind life's experiences and to embrace the beauty of the journey.

My mistake: I went through life not trusting as much as I should. I allowed anxiety and work to lead parts of my life without fully understanding what had been given to me and how lucky I was.

Chapter 3.1

Trust the Process, My Friend, Trust the Process

You live long enough, you start learning that trust is key. You learn that if you don't trust yourself, no one will trust you, and if you don't trust the process, you will suffer. I had this ritual after 2016 to go on the Camino de Santiago pilgrimage in Spain. I have done it about eight times by the time I am writing this book—had to skip a few years due to COVID—yet it was never easy.

The Camino de Santiago, or Way of St. James, is a historic pilgrimage route leading to the cathedral of Santiago de Compostela in Galicia, Spain, where the remains of Saint James are believed to be buried. Dating back to the 9th century, it remains a popular journey for spiritual, cultural, and personal reasons. The most traveled route, the Camino Francés, begins in St. Jean Pied de Port, France, stretching about 780 kilometers. Pilgrims, known for their camaraderie, stay in hostels and collect stamps in a "credential" to earn a "Compostela" upon completion. The pilgrimage offers a profound blend of physical challenge and spiritual reward, traversing diverse landscapes and historic sites.

When I shared that I did this with friends and family, they used to always mention, "Oh, I must have gotten so used to it." But the truth is, I never did. You see, it was a huge contrast, living in North America, which is a culture ruled by law and restriction, and going to the other side of the ocean to experience true freedom. It was tough—not sure about you, but for me, every time I used to travel, I needed to get used to whatever location I was traveling to.

Let's say I just came back from a trip from Spain. I've already gotten used to the pace of life, the food, the culture, how people work, how people rest, how people sleep after lunch. I've gotten so used to their culture and their siesta, so by the time I'm back in Canada, and the pace of life is much faster, it's a bit hard to adapt. The first week is never easy; the second week is better, and the third week, you're just so used to it, it becomes the new normal.

And the same works the other way around. Let's say I'm planning to go to Spain, and I'm excited to go on my Camino de Santiago, but then just before I travel, I start realizing how much of a change it's going to be, and the fact that I couldn't fully divorce from my work right away, and that my clients have certain expectations and certain rules, and these expectations have to be met.

So just before traveling on my trip to Spain, I started realizing that it was going to be an ordeal. It's a matter of getting used to the other culture again. It is time to work from anywhere I can, with the time that I have, and it's time for me to find a new place to sleep every night, to find a bicycle that I can use on my trip, to find food that I need to eat, whether in the morning, at noon, or at night. It's a lot to juggle all the time. And the moment you start worrying, worrying never stops. If you're worried about one thing, then you're going to be reminded of another thing that you forgot to worry about, and it becomes a very vicious cycle.

Yet you have to trust the process, my friend. You have to trust God, you have to trust the universe, you have to trust Jesus, you have to trust Allah. You have to put your trust in a higher power, you have to put trust in the decision that you are making, that it's guided by your intuition, which is in turn guided by God. You have to remember that whatever you're doing, you're doing it for the greater good, you're doing it to better yourself, you're doing it to enjoy life more, and it's a worthwhile cause. Not only is it a worthwhile cause, it's going to make your life worth living. Because without these trips, without these adventures, without discovering things through your own eyes and accepting the beauty of the world, then what is there to live for?

To prove this point a bit more for you, every single time I go on this trip, I get to meet a new angel. I get to meet someone along the way very early on who welcomes me, loves me, takes care of me, doesn't ask me for anything in return, gives me free directions, gives me their sandwich, gives me their food, gives me their love. I meet an angel every single time I go on the Camino de Santiago. I meet an angel every time I go out of my comfort zone.

I realize that these angels are in my life every day, especially where I'm at, where I live, in my home in Canada. These angels are the people that are around me, except that I'm less grateful for them here than I am when I'm extremely uncomfortable in another country. Let me tell you this: every time I go on the Camino de Santiago, sometimes I run into someone I already know, such as Christina from Villafranca del Bierzo, who takes me in, gives me accommodation, cooks food for me, allows me to shower, does my laundry, and sends me off all taken care of. Every time I leave her place, I cry for a few hours while I'm biking.

Believe it or not, I cry shamelessly. Initially, it's an uphill heading towards Burgos, and on that highway, sometimes the wind is so strong that I can hardly stand, let alone pedal. Yet, I cry for hours. It's not tears of sadness, but tears of gratitude. Tears for having someone like her in my life who, without knowing me, takes care of me, and gives me more love than I deserve. It's the most humbling feeling I can ever describe.

And as I'm heading towards the city of Burgos, I always realize that it's time for me to stop the worrying and start enjoying the journey. It's time for me to start trusting the process. After all, every single time, there's always an angel waiting for me. There's always someone who's going to take care of me. There's always going to be a hand that's going to help me. That's what I trust in this journey. That's what I trust in life.

And after I leave her place and head towards my destination, I always remember that the tears of gratitude that I shed are always followed by tears of joy. The reason I'm telling you this story is that I want you to know that trust is the key to a meaningful and fulfilling life. Trust is the key to moving forward, whether it's in your career, your relationships, your dreams, or your aspirations. Trust the process, my friend. Trust it deeply and unconditionally, because without trust, there's nothing but fear and worry.

Chapter 3.2

Something Has Been Given to You: Life

Life is a precious gift, one that is often taken for granted. Every moment, every breath, every experience is something given to you, not something that is owed to you. The sooner you understand this, the more meaningful your life will become. When you recognize life as a gift, you start to appreciate the little things, the small joys, and the simple pleasures that come your way.

I've seen many people who live their lives as if they are owed something as if the world owes them happiness, success, and fulfillment. But the truth is, the world owes us nothing. Life is a gift, and it's up to us to make the most of it. We are not entitled to anything beyond what we have, and even what we have can be taken away in an instant. The sooner we realize this, the sooner we can start living with a sense of gratitude and appreciation for the life we've been given.

I used to be one of those people who thought that life owed me something. I believed that because I worked hard, was a good person, and did the right things, life should reward me with success, happiness, and all I desired. But life doesn't work that way. It's not a transaction where you put in something and get something back in return. Life is a gift, and it's up to us to cherish it, to make the most of it, and to find joy in the journey.

When I started seeing life as a gift, everything changed. I stopped worrying so much about what I didn't have and started appreciating what I did have. I stopped focusing on the things that went wrong and started celebrating the things that went right. I started to see every challenge, every obstacle, every setback as an opportunity to learn, to grow, and to become a better version of myself.

Life is a gift, my friend. It's not something that is given to everyone, and it's not something that will last forever. It's a fleeting moment in time, a brief opportunity to make a difference, to leave a mark, to create something beautiful. Don't waste it. Don't take it for granted. Live it fully, live it deeply, and live it with gratitude.

Chapter 3.3

The Sun Will Always Shine

Remember that the sun will always shine again, no matter how dark the times may seem. This metaphor serves as a reminder that bad times are temporary. Embrace optimism and hope, knowing that better days are ahead. This resilience and positive outlook are crucial to maintaining happiness through life's challenges. I can guarantee you one thing: the sun will always shine. One of the prayers I do every morning is to look at the sun, and I thank it for being there every day. We seem to take it for granted. It's been there with us from the beginning, all of us. And just when the night is the darkest before dawn, it crawls in and brings light and warmth into our lives. We've all been in the darkest hour: one-third helpless, one-third hopeless, and one-third pointless. We've all been there when all hope is lost, when we can't bring someone back, when we just can't bring a moment back. Trust me, I lost my dog this year. I lost many people in my life. I don't think anything compares to or will ever compare to losing Coco. May she rest in peace. I was the person for that dog. You know, every dog has a human. I was that human. I loved Coco more than anything and still love her now more than ever. I cannot help but cry every time I think about her. When I lost Coco, I didn't even know what to do. I didn't even know where to start. It was a freak accident with one of our neighbours who was taking care of her. All of this is to say that by the time I was back in Montreal, Coco was already cold and gone. I went to see her in the hospital, and every time I saw her before, she was full of joy and love. She used to run to me, and I used to pet her for 10 minutes every time I saw her, and she still wanted more. But at that moment in the hospital, she was just a cold body lying on a bench. It was the 2nd of January 2024. It's already cold, windy, and dark that time of year, so having to deal with the news as such usually kills you and will make the toughest man cry. Throughout all this uncertainty and hardships, I was always hopeful. I knew that whatever decisions I was going to have to make within that week right after Coco's death would affect the rest of my life, and I had to stay positive. All this to say is that I always believed, never doubted the sun would shine again, and always had to hope for the best. This was an actual test of my faith and belief, and I knew that by hoping for the best, I would get the best. A week later, I drove outside Montreal for two and a half hours and picked up Biscotti, a white golden retriever. She fills my life with happiness, joy, and growth; I can't imagine a life without her. Many people told me, "Tarek, you're making an emotional decision," and I would say, "I wish all my decisions were as emotional as this one."

Chapter 3.4

Look at the Gift in Everything

There's a gift in everything, even in the challenges and hardships you face. Life is full of unexpected twists and turns; not all are pleasant. But if you look closely, you'll find that every experience, every setback, every problematic moment comes with a hidden gift—a lesson, a blessing, or an opportunity for growth.

I remember a time when I was going through a particularly rough patch. I had just experienced a significant personal and professional loss, and it felt like the ground had been pulled out from under me. Everything I had worked for, everything I had believed in, seemed to be crumbling. I was angry, hurt, and lost.

I couldn't understand why this was happening to me, why life was so unfair.

But as time passed and the initial shock began to wear off, I started to see things differently. As painful as it was, I realized that this experience had a purpose. It taught me something, pushing me to grow in ways I hadn't anticipated. It forced me to reevaluate my priorities, question what really mattered in my life, and make changes that I might never have made otherwise.

In hindsight, I can see that this challenging time was a gift. It didn't feel like one then, and I certainly didn't welcome it with open arms. But looking back, I can see how it shaped me, how it made me stronger, more resilient, and more compassionate. It helped me develop a deeper sense of empathy for others going through difficult times and gave me a new perspective on what it means to live a meaningful life.

There's a gift in everything, even in moments of pain and suffering. It's not always easy to see; sometimes it takes time to uncover, but it's there. The next time you find yourself facing a difficult situation, try to shift your perspective. Instead of asking, "Why is this happening to me?" ask, "What is the gift in this? What can I learn from this? How can this experience help me grow?"

By looking for the gift in everything, you'll begin to see life in a new light. You'll start to appreciate the journey, with all its ups and downs, and you'll find that even the toughest times can bring unexpected blessings. Life is a gift, and within it, there are countless other gifts waiting to be discovered.

Let me share a story about Mark, on an entrepreneurial friend of mine:

Mark was the kind of person you couldn't help but root for. A few years ago, he quit his comfortable corporate job to chase his dream of launching a startup. It was a bold move, especially with a young family to support, but Mark was passionate and driven. He had a clear vision of what he wanted to create—a platform that would revolutionize the way small businesses managed their finances.

For the first year, everything seemed to be going well. Mark assembled a small but talented team, secured some initial funding, and started to build his product. The excitement was palpable every time we caught up. He would talk for hours about the possibilities, the potential, and the impact he believed his startup could have.

But as the months went on, the challenges began to mount. The initial funding started to dry up faster than expected, and the product development hit several unexpected roadblocks. Features that were supposed to be simple turned out to be complicated, and the team was stretched thin. To make matters worse, a key investor backed out just as they were about to launch the product.

Mark was devastated. He had poured everything into this startup—his time, his energy, his savings. Now, it felt like it was all falling apart. He tried to stay optimistic, but it was clear that the strain was taking its toll. The sleepless nights, the constant stress, and the fear of failure loomed large.

One evening, after yet another day of setbacks, Mark called me. I could hear the exhaustion in his voice, the frustration, the doubt. "I don't know if I can do this anymore," he admitted. "Maybe I've just been fooling myself. Maybe I should have stayed in my safe job."

I listened as he vented, knowing that he needed to let it all out. When he was done, I said, "Mark, I get it. This is tough. It's brutal, even. But have you thought about what this experience might be teaching you?"

He was silent for a moment, probably thinking I was about to launch into some motivational speech that wouldn't actually help. But I continued, "Look, I'm not saying this to sugarcoat anything. What you're going through is incredibly hard. But maybe there's something in this struggle that could be valuable—something that you wouldn't have learned if everything had gone perfectly."

Mark sighed, "Like what? How to fail?"

"Maybe," I said gently, "but also how to adapt, how to lead under pressure, how to stay resilient when things don't go your way. These are lessons you can't learn from success alone. They're forged in the fire of these exact moments."

Over the next few weeks, Mark didn't magically find a solution to all his problems. The investor didn't suddenly come back, and the product didn't miraculously finish itself. But something shifted in him. He started to see the challenges not just as obstacles, but as opportunities to learn and grow.

He re-evaluated his approach, streamlined the product, and focused on what was truly essential. He also reached out to his network, not for more funding, but for advice and mentorship. To his surprise, many of the people he contacted had faced similar challenges in their own careers. They shared their stories, their failures, and how those failures had ultimately led to their greatest successes.

Gradually, Mark's mindset began to change. He stopped viewing the startup's struggles as a sign of impending failure and started seeing them as part of the journey. He realized that the setbacks were teaching him how to be a better leader, a more effective problem-solver, and a more compassionate person.

Eventually, Mark's startup did launch, albeit later and with fewer features than initially planned. It wasn't the blockbuster success he had once dreamed of, but it found its niche and started to grow steadily. More importantly, Mark emerged from the experience with a new perspective.

One evening, over a much-needed beer, Mark said to me, "You know, I wouldn't wish those tough times on anyone, but I wouldn't trade them either. They taught me more than any success ever could. There really is a gift in everything, even when it's hard to see at the time."

I smiled, knowing that Mark had discovered something far more valuable than immediate success. He had found resilience, wisdom, and the ability to find the hidden gifts in life's challenges. And that, I knew, would serve him in whatever came next.

We Make Mistakes, Mistakes Make Us

" Poem

"Compass Within." – by Tarek Riman

In a world of noise and blinding light,
Where shadows dance and truths seem slight,
There lies within, a compass true,
A guide to show what you must do.

When doubts arise and paths confuse,
And whispers tell you which to choose,
Remember this, your heart's own voice,
Will always lead to the right choice.

For discipline, though hard and stern,
Is not a flame meant just to burn.
It molds, it shapes, it sets you free,
Unlocks the strength within, the key.

Triumph may come, or disaster fall,
But treat them both, impostors all.
For neither can your worth define,
It's how you walk, not where you climb.

Stand firm when winds of change do blow,
And trust the light inside to grow.
For in the end, it's not the gain,
But how you danced amid the rain.

So listen close, with humble ear,
To voices far, to those held dear.
The compass points, the path you tread,
Leads to a life fulfilled, well-spread.

We Make Mistakes, Mistakes Make Us

No fear to start, no shame in fall,
For strength is found in rising tall.
In every step, a lesson learned,
In every flame, a fire burned.

The world may press, may try to sway,
But hold your course, don't lose your way.
For deep within, a voice will sing,
Of discipline's unyielding ring.

And when you doubt, when shadows creep,
Remember in the dark, you leap.
With courage bold, and heart alight,
You'll find what's good, you'll know what's right.

Chapter 4
Discipline

Summary:

In a world saturated with noise and conflicting messages, discerning what is truly good and right can be challenging. However, deep within us, we all possess an inner compass that can guide us if we take the time to listen. This chapter emphasizes the importance of aligning with your core values and staying true to what you know is right, even when external pressures try to sway you. Making the right choices often requires courage and integrity, especially when the path ahead is difficult. Ultimately, living in accordance with what is good and right leads to a life of meaning, fulfillment, and respect for oneself and others.

My Mistake: I used to see discipline as my kryptonite, a burden that held me back. But over time, I realized that discipline wasn't my enemy—it was the key to unlocking my potential, something I needed to embrace rather than resist.

Chapter 4.1

Know What Is Good and Right

In a world filled with constant noise and conflicting messages, it can be difficult to know what is truly good and right. We are bombarded with opinions, beliefs, and values from all sides, and it's easy to become overwhelmed or confused about what we should believe or how we should act. But deep down, each of us has an inner compass, a sense of what is good and right, that can guide us if we take the time to listen to it.

Throughout my life, I've faced many situations where I was unsure of what to do or how to act. I've made decisions that I later regretted because I didn't take the time to reflect on what was truly good and right. Instead, I allowed myself to be influenced by external pressures, by what others expected of me, or _y own fears and insecurities. But whenever I took the time to quiet my mind, to tune out the noise, and to listen to my inner voice, I found that I always knew, deep down, what the right thing to do was.

Knowing what is good and right doesn't always mean that the path ahead will be easy. In fact, it often means making difficult choices, standing up for what you believe in, or going against the grain. But it's these choices that define your character, that shape who you are as a person, and that ultimately lead to a life of integrity and fulfillment.

One of the most important lessons I've learned is that doing what is good and right isn't about being perfect or never making mistakes. It's about being honest with yourself, owning up to your mistakes, and striving to do better. It's about living in alignment with your values, treating others with kindness and respect, and making decisions that reflect the kind of person you want to be.

In a world that often values success and achievement over integrity and character, it's easy to lose sight of what is truly important. But I believe that at the end of the day, what matters most is not how much you've accomplished but how you've lived your life. Have you treated others with compassion? Have you acted with integrity? Have you made choices that align with your values and beliefs?

Take the time to reflect on what is good and right in your life. Tune out the noise, the distractions, the opinions of others, and listen to your inner voice. Trust that you have the wisdom within you to know what is good and right, and let that guide your actions and decisions. It's not always easy, but it's the path that leads to a life of meaning, purpose, and true fulfillment.

Let me share a very recent story.

I was teaching a class at one of the top universities in Canada and introduced a leaderboard to gamify activities. It kept students engaged in an age of short attention spans. This worked for years until a coordinator attended my class and gave feedback, saying someone found the leaderboard aggressive and preferred a more positive experience.

I was shocked and speechless. The coordinator said to keep the leaderboard but to let students down easy. I questioned how students would learn if there was no clear right or wrong. We need to know what's right and wrong to move forward in life. Without it, we're lost.

I kept the leaderboard and continued saying "no" when necessary. As a teacher, I prioritize integrity and care.

In life, you need to understand what's good and bad, right and wrong. Often, people won't tell us these truths for the sake of conformity, so we owe it to ourselves to know. I set a compass for myself, asking if God, my grandmother, or my ancestors were watching, would they be proud? This has never failed me.

Find your compass or use mine. Critical thinking and discernment are essential for navigating life's complexities. Distinguishing between what is good or bad, beneficial or harmful, requires understanding your values, goals, and context. This helps you make informed decisions that support your growth and happiness.

Chapter 4.2

Accept Triumph and Disaster

Rudyard Kipling once wrote in his poem "If—": "If you can meet with Triumph and Disaster / And treat those two impostors just the same." This line has always resonated with me, as it captures the essence of what it means to navigate life's ups and downs with grace and resilience.

Triumph and disaster are two sides of the same coin, both inevitable parts of the human experience. Yet, we often react to them in very different ways. Triumph is usually met with celebration, pride, and a sense of accomplishment, while disaster can bring feelings of despair, frustration, and defeat. But Kipling's words remind us that both triumph and disaster are fleeting moments, not permanent states. They are impostors in the sense that they do not define who we are or determine our worth.

Over the years, I've had my fair share of triumphs and disasters. I've experienced the highs of success, the satisfaction of achieving a long-sought goal, the joy of seeing hard work pay off. But I've also faced the lows of failure, the pain of setbacks, and the disappointment of things not going as planned. What I've learned is that it's important not to get too attached to either triumph or disaster. Both will pass, and life will continue to move forward.

When you achieve something great, it's natural to feel proud and to celebrate your success. But it's also important to stay grounded, to remember that this moment of triumph is just one chapter in your life's story. Don't let it inflate your ego or make you complacent. Keep striving, keep pushing yourself, and keep working towards new goals.

On the other hand, when disaster strikes, it's easy to feel like the world is crumbling around you. But it's in these moments that your true character is tested. How you respond to disaster says a lot about who you are. Do you give up, or do you find the strength to keep going? Do you wallow in self-pity, or do you learn from the experience and grow stronger?

Kipling's advice to treat triumph and disaster just the same is a reminder to maintain perspective. Neither triumph nor disaster should define you. What matters is how you handle them, how you learn from them, and how you move forward. Life is full of highs and lows, and the key is to navigate them with equanimity, grace, and resilience.

Accept triumph with humility and disaster with courage. Embrace the lessons that both have to offer, and remember that they are just moments in time, not the sum total of who you are. By keeping this perspective, you can maintain a sense of balance and inner peace, no matter what life throws your way.

Let me tell you a story.

There was one mountain in particular that stood out—the highest mountain in Lebanon, Qurnat as Sawda'. It was said that few had ever reached its summit, and those who did returned changed, carrying with them a sense of accomplishment that few could understand. As a young man, full of ambition and eager to prove myself, I became obsessed with the idea of climbing that mountain. It wasn't just about the physical challenge; it was about proving something to myself, about showing that I had what it took to conquer something truly formidable.

So, one summer, I decided it was time. I prepared for weeks, gathering supplies, training my body, and steeling my mind for the journey ahead. When the day came, I left early in the morning, the sun just beginning to rise over the horizon, casting a golden light on the path that lay before me.

The climb was as difficult as I had imagined— perhaps even more so. The air grew thinner with each step, and the path became increasingly treacherous. But I was determined. I kept going, driven by the thought of standing at the summit, looking out over the world from the highest point in Lebanon.

Finally, after hours of climbing, I reached the peak. The view was unlike anything I had ever seen—the valleys and villages spread out far below, the sky so close it felt like I could reach out and touch it. I felt a surge of triumph, a sense of accomplishment so powerful that it made all the effort, all the struggles, worth it. I had done it. I had conquered the highest mountain in Lebanon.

But just as I was savoring that moment, the weather began to change. A sudden storm rolled in, the clouds darkening the sky, the wind picking up with a ferocity that took me by surprise. The once-stable ground beneath my feet seemed to shift, and in an instant, the triumph I had felt was replaced by fear. The mountain, which had just moments before seemed to bow to my will, now felt like a powerful force, indifferent to my achievements, ready to swallow me whole.

As I struggled to find shelter, to protect myself from the storm that threatened to overwhelm me, a lesson that my father had often shared with me came rushing back: "If you can meet with Triumph and Disaster, and treat those two impostors just the same…"

In that moment, I understood the wisdom in those words. Triumph and disaster—they are both fleeting, both impostors that can easily mislead us if we let them. The true test of character is not in how we handle success or failure, but in how we remain grounded, how we continue to move forward with integrity and purpose, regardless of what life throws our way.

I managed to find a small crevice in the rock, where I waited out the storm. When it finally passed, I made my way back down the mountain, the experience lingering in my mind. The climb had changed me, but not in the way I had expected. It wasn't the triumph of reaching the summit that stayed with me; it was the realization that neither victory nor defeat defines us. What defines us is our resilience, our ability to meet whatever comes our way with calm and steady resolve.

Now, years later, as I stand before my students in Montreal, I often think back to that climb in Lebanon. I share the story with them, hoping to impart the lesson I learned on that mountain. Life will always present us with triumphs and disasters, but we must remember that they are both temporary, both just moments in time. What truly matters is how we respond, how we choose to move forward, and how we maintain our sense of self in the face of it all. Stay humble.

Research Late at Night, Make Decisions in the Morning

I've always found that my best ideas and insights come late at night. There's something about the quiet solitude of the late hours that allows my mind to wander, to explore new ideas, to think creatively. It's a time when the distractions of the day have faded away, and I can focus on what truly matters. But while the late-night hours are great for research and brainstorming, I've learned that it's best to wait until the morning to make any major decisions.

Late at night, our minds are often in a different state. We're more relaxed, more open to possibilities, more willing to take risks. This can be a great thing when it comes to exploring new ideas, but it can also lead to impulsive decisions that we might regret in the light of day. That's why I've made it a rule to sleep on any big decisions and to revisit them in the morning when my mind is fresh and clear.

There's something about the clarity of the morning that brings perspective. After a good night's sleep, I find that I can see things more objectively, weigh the pros and cons more carefully, and make decisions with a clearer head. What seemed like a brilliant idea at midnight might not hold up so well in the light of day, and that's okay. It's all part of the process of making thoughtful, informed decisions.

If you're like me and do some of your best thinking late at night, I encourage you to embrace that time for research, brainstorming, and exploring new ideas. But before you make any major decisions, give yourself the time and space to sleep on it and revisit it in the morning. You'll find that your decisions are more grounded, more thoughtful, and more likely to lead to positive outcomes.

Let me share a story.

It was well past midnight in my Montreal apartment, and the city outside was quiet. The only sounds were the occasional hum of a car passing by and the soft ticking of the clock on my wall. I had been staring at my laptop screen for hours, my eyes burning from the strain, but my mind was still racing. I was deep into research for a new project—one that could significantly impact my business. The pressure was on, and I could feel it in every muscle of my body.

The project was complex, involving multiple variables and potential risks. I had been gathering data, analyzing trends, and brainstorming strategies for weeks. Tonight, I was trying to piece it all together, hoping that some late-night inspiration would strike. But the more I pushed myself, the more muddled my thoughts became. I could feel the familiar tug of exhaustion creeping in, but I ignored it, telling myself I just needed a little more time to figure it all out.

Hours passed, and by the time I looked at the clock again, it was nearly 3 AM. My brain was foggy, and every new idea seemed to dissolve into a sea of uncertainty. Frustrated, I leaned back in my chair, rubbing my eyes and taking a deep breath. I knew I was at my limit, but

I couldn't shake the feeling that I was missing something—some crucial piece of the puzzle that would make everything click.

Just then, I remembered something a mentor once told me: "Never make important decisions at night. Do your research, but sleep on it before you decide anything." At the time, it seemed like simple advice, but tonight, it felt like a lifeline.

Reluctantly, I shut down my laptop and stood up, stretching my stiff limbs. The idea of going to bed when I felt so close to a breakthrough was tough, but I also knew that pushing myself any further wouldn't help. So, I made a deal with myself: I would let it go for the night, get some rest, and revisit everything in the morning with fresh eyes.

I climbed into bed, my mind still buzzing with thoughts, but as soon as my head hit the pillow, the exhaustion took over. I drifted off to sleep, my brain finally getting the rest it needed.

The next morning, I woke up to the soft light of the sun filtering through my window. The anxiety and frustration of the previous night were gone, replaced by a sense of clarity. I brewed a cup of coffee and sat back down at my desk, opening my laptop to the same project that had seemed so overwhelming just hours before.

As I began reviewing my notes, something amazing happened. The ideas that had been tangled and confusing the night before now seemed to align effortlessly. It was as if my brain had sorted through the chaos while I slept, organizing the information into a clear, logical pattern. What had felt impossible in the early hours now seemed manageable, even exciting.

I started making notes, refining my strategy with a renewed sense of purpose. Decisions that had seemed daunting were now straightforward, and I could see the path forward more clearly than ever. The solution had been there all along—I just needed to give my mind the space to process it.

By the time I finished, I felt a sense of satisfaction that I hadn't felt in weeks. The project, which had once felt like a mountain I couldn't climb, now seemed like an opportunity—a challenge I was ready to tackle head-on. And it all came down to one simple decision: to step back, rest, and let my mind do its work in the background.

That day, as I went about my tasks, I kept thinking about how close I'd come to making hasty decisions in the dead of night, driven by exhaustion and stress. But by giving myself the time to rest and approach the problem with a clear head, I was able to see things in a new light, make better decisions, and ultimately set myself up for success.

From that point on, I made it a rule: research late at night if you must, but always make decisions in the morning. The clarity that comes with a fresh mind is invaluable, and sometimes, the best thing you can do is step away, trust the process, and let the answers come to you when the time is right.

Chapter 4.4

Worn out tools

My grandpa used to say: "If you watch everything you worked for burn and get destroyed, clean off the dust, dust yourself off, and stand up and rebuild everything once again with worn-out and destroyed tools, then you have everything in this world."

In no shape or form was I born from privilege. Every family member, including myself, has witnessed war in its ugliest form. Every family member had to work through the ground, and we all have seen our fair share of suffering.

But I'll tell you one thing: we had a good example to look up to.

As we witness multiple wars, you start living with the fact that electricity is a scarcity and a privilege, not a right you should have, and so is hot water.

Knowing that very well, my granddad used to leave the hose in the garden during the day, especially on hot summer days, and he would throw it on the red Mediterranean soil in his garden. As the sun set, he would look at us and say, "Kids, it's fine for you to shower." My grandma would hand us her homemade soap, which is made out of olive oil, and my grandpa would take the same hose that was out in the sun all day, full of boiling water, and he would turn the water up slowly while we washed our bodies off outside as young kids, with the sun setting in the background. A tear comes into my eye, not because we felt poor, we never knew what poor felt like, but because I lost both my grandparents, and this beautiful moment cannot be relived ever again.

My grandpa, my dad, and my uncle used to fix everything with very worn-out tools. Nothing was new;

everything was either donated, built from scratch, or repurposed for a new use.

In my early twenties, I stepped away, moved to North America, and got everything new. Everything was fresh; everything was available at my fingertips. All I had to do was pay a bit, and I had the best and latest tools available at my fingertips.

But something changed when I had it all within reach. The ease and convenience of modern life were undeniably appealing, yet I found myself missing something deeper. I realized that the true value wasn't in having the newest, shiniest tools but in the resourcefulness, resilience, and ingenuity that my family had instilled in me. Those worn-out tools, passed down through generations, carried with them the lessons of perseverance and the spirit of making do with what you have—lessons that no amount of money or technology could replace.

Now, as I navigate life with access to all the conveniences that the modern world offers, I hold onto those memories and lessons. The discipline of planning, the determination to rebuild when things fall apart, and the resilience to face life's challenges are qualities that my family exemplified daily, often under the harshest conditions. These are the qualities that truly define success—not the tools themselves, but the hands that wield them and the mind that directs them.

Every morning, as I sit down to structure my day, I think of my grandfather carefully laying out that garden hose, making the best of what he had, and creating a moment of comfort in a world that often offered little. I remind myself that no matter how advanced the tools at my disposal are, it's the mindset and discipline I bring to my work that will ultimately make the difference.

Starting each day with a well-structured plan rooted in thoughtful preparation is my way of honoring those lessons. It's about transforming the raw materials of life—whether they're shiny and new or worn and weathered—into something meaningful. And when life inevitably knocks everything down, I know that I have the strength to dust myself off, pick up those worn-out tools, and start rebuilding. Because at the end of the day, it's not the tools that define us, but the resilience, creativity, and determination to keep moving forward, no matter what.

Chapter 4.5

Ask, and You Will Only Ask a Stupid Question Once

One of the biggest barriers to learning and growth is the fear of asking questions, especially the fear of asking what we perceive as a "stupid" question. We worry that asking a question will make us look ignorant, inexperienced, or incompetent. But in reality, the only stupid question is the one that's never asked.

When you ask a question, even if it seems simple or basic, you're opening yourself up to learning, to understanding, and to improving. You're acknowledging that you don't know everything—and that's okay. No one expects you to know everything, and in fact, the people who are most successful are often the ones who aren't afraid to ask questions, to seek out knowledge, and to admit when they don't know something.

I've found that the fear of asking questions is often rooted in pride or insecurity. We don't want to appear vulnerable or less capable in front of others. But this fear is misplaced. In most cases, people are more than willing to help, to share their knowledge, and to answer your questions. And once you ask, you'll never have to ask that "stupid" question again.

I remember early in my career, there were times when I didn't ask questions because I was afraid of looking foolish. I thought I was supposed to know everything, to have all the answers, and I didn't want to show any weakness. But this attitude held me back. It kept me from learning, from growing, and from gaining the knowledge I needed to succeed.

It wasn't until I started asking questions—lots of questions—that I really began to grow. I realized that asking questions was a sign of strength, not weakness.

It showed that I was curious, that I wanted to learn, that I was committed to improving. And as I started asking more questions, I found that people respected me more, not less. They saw me as someone who was engaged, who was eager to learn, and who wasn't afraid to admit when I didn't know something.

So don't be afraid to ask questions, no matter how simple or basic they may seem. It's the only way to learn, to grow, and to get the answers you need. And remember, you only have to ask a "stupid" question once—after that, you'll know the answer, and you'll be better for it.

Let me share a story.

I was teaching a class a few years ago, and I had to create an exam. The exam had three questions. Two questions were worth 25 marks each, and the last one was worth 50 marks. The exam was clearly written, and it was emailed to all students beforehand. The questions were not provided, of course, but the time of the exam was, and all the details related to it.

The night before the exam, I was contacted by one of my students who didn't attend most of the classes throughout the term. He was emailing me asking what the exam would be about and what questions he should study for. I didn't respond to his email, not out of spite, but I just didn't have time, and I don't have time to create a new exam for him.

I created the exam for the students who came to class. I created the exam for the students who took notes. I created the exam for the students who put in the time and effort and the dedication to learn the material, and I wasn't going to create another one for one student who just emailed me at the last minute.

What the student didn't realize is that he should have asked much earlier in the term. What the student didn't realize is that he was a bit too late for that. What the student didn't realize is that he just made his life much more complicated because he was too shy or afraid or too proud to ask questions earlier in the term.

Every time I see a student, every time I see someone who is afraid to ask questions, every time I see someone who's afraid to speak up, I realize that there's a problem, a much bigger problem.

One of the chapters that I teach in one of my courses is on self-awareness. I always ask my students to put the questions out there to the community, to the greater group, so everybody can learn from them.

One of the things that I do with my students when I teach is, for example, I ask them to build a business, and building a business, there are a lot of questions to ask. One of the questions is, "How do we do market research?" "What questions do we ask in our surveys?" "How do we build a financial model?" "How do we build our spreadsheets?"

Every time I asked the students to ask these questions, I noticed that the more questions they asked, the better they got at asking questions. And every time they asked a question, they realized that they were not the only ones wondering. They realized that they were not the only ones who had that question, and they realized that it was much easier to share the answers to the questions with the group.

When you ask a question, you will only ask a stupid question once.

When you ask a question, you will realize that you are actually much smarter than you thought, because the question that you ask is not a stupid question, but it's a question that's been asked by a lot of people, but no one has the courage to ask.

The moment you ask a question, you will only ask a stupid question once, and that's it. You will get the answer. You will move on, and you will learn.

Chapter 4.6

Learn and Avoid Going to the School of Hard Knocks

Experience is often touted as the best teacher, but it doesn't always have to be your own experience. The school of hard knocks—learning from your own mistakes, struggles, and failures—can be a tough and painful way to gain wisdom. While it's true that you can learn a great deal from your own experiences, it's also important to recognize that you can learn just as much, if not more, from the experiences of others.

One of the most valuable lessons I've learned is the importance of seeking out knowledge and advice from those who have walked the path before me. Whether it's through books, mentors, or simply listening to the stories of others, there's a wealth of wisdom available to us if we're willing to learn from it. By learning from the successes and failures of others, you can avoid many of the pitfalls and mistakes that would otherwise come your way.

I've seen people who insist on learning everything the hard way, who refuse to take advice or seek guidance, believing that they need to figure it all out on their own. While there's something to be said for the value of personal experience, there's also a great deal of wisdom in avoiding unnecessary hardships by learning from the experiences of others.

When I look back on my own life, I realize that many of the challenges I faced could have been avoided if I had been more willing to listen to the advice of others. I was often too stubborn, too proud, or too convinced of my own way of doing things to see the value in learning from others. But as I've grown older, I've come to understand that true wisdom comes not just from our own experiences, but from the collective experiences of those who have come before us.

So, take the time to seek out mentors, to read books, to listen to the stories of those who have faced similar challenges. Learn from their successes and their failures, and apply those lessons to your own life. It doesn't mean that you won't make mistakes or face challenges, but it does mean that you can navigate those challenges with greater wisdom and foresight.

The school of hard knocks can be a harsh and unforgiving teacher. But by being open to learning from others, you can avoid many of the hard lessons and move forward with greater confidence and clarity.

Let me share a tough story with you.

When I was in my early twenties, I thought I knew everything. I had just moved to Montreal, full of ambition and dreams, ready to take on the world. I believed that success was just around the corner and that I could figure everything out on my own. Like many people my age, I was convinced that I didn't need anyone's advice—I was determined to learn by doing, even if it meant making a few mistakes along the way.

Back then, I had just started my first business. It was a digital marketing agency, a field I was passionate about but still relatively new to. I had studied the basics in school, read countless books, and watched videos online, but I hadn't yet faced the real-world challenges that come with running a business. Despite the warnings from more experienced friends and mentors, I was confident that I could handle it.

One of the first major projects I took on was with a large client, a deal that could catapult my business to the next level. The stakes were high, and the pressure was even higher. I threw myself into the project, working long hours, managing a small team, and trying to meet every one of the client's demands. I was determined to prove myself.

But as the project progressed, things started to unravel. The client's expectations kept shifting, and I found myself constantly scrambling to keep up. I made decisions without fully understanding the consequences, took on more work than I could handle, and refused to ask for help. I thought that showing any sign of weakness would be a failure.

Before I knew it, the project was in serious trouble. Deadlines were missed, the quality of work wasn't up to standard, and the client was getting frustrated. I was too deep into the project to back out, but I didn't know how to fix the mess I had created. I felt like I was drowning, and for the first time, I realized that I was in over my head.

One evening, after yet another exhausting day, I sat in my tiny apartment, staring at my laptop, overwhelmed with stress. I thought about all the advice I had ignored—the mentors who had told me to start small, the colleagues who had warned me about taking on too much too soon, and the friends who had offered their support. I had chosen to go it alone, thinking I had something to prove, but now I was paying the price.

I decided to call one of my mentors, someone I had admired but kept at arm's length because I didn't want to seem like I needed help. When he picked up, I told him everything—how the project was falling apart, how I was struggling to manage it all, and how I didn't know what to do next.

He listened patiently, and when I finished, he said something that has stuck with me ever since. "Tarek," he said, "there's no shame in asking for help. The smartest people in the world know when to seek advice. You don't have to learn everything the hard way."

He then offered some practical advice—how to renegotiate the project's scope, how to delegate tasks more effectively, and how to communicate better with the client. His words were like a lifeline, giving me the clarity I desperately needed. I realized that I didn't have to face these challenges alone, and that seeking guidance didn't make me weak—it made me smarter.

Over the next few weeks, I applied his advice, slowly turning the project around. I worked closely with my team, set clearer boundaries with the client, and focused on delivering what was realistic instead of trying to meet every demand. It wasn't easy, and there were still bumps along the way, but eventually, we completed the project to the client's satisfaction.

That experience taught me a lesson I'll never forget: you don't always have to go to the school of hard knocks. Learning from others—whether it's through their successes or their mistakes—can save you a lot of pain and setbacks. While some lessons do come from personal experience, many can be learned by listening to those who have walked the path before you.

From that day on, I made it a point to seek advice whenever I faced a challenge. I built a network of mentors, colleagues, and friends who I could turn to for guidance. And most importantly, I learned to put my ego aside and recognize that I didn't have to have all the answers.

Looking back, I'm grateful for that early failure because it taught me the value of learning from others. The school of hard knocks may be effective, but it's also costly. By being open to advice and learning from the experiences of those who have been there before, I've been able to navigate the ups and downs of life and business with a lot less unnecessary pain.

And now, when I see someone younger or less experienced struggling, I try to offer the same advice I once received. It's not about avoiding mistakes altogether—it's about making sure that when you do fall, you don't fall as hard or as often. Because at the end of the day, the smartest move you can make is to learn from those who've already been through the fire, so you don't have to get burned the same way.

Chapter 4.7

Always Get a Rough First Draft, Don't Wait Too Long

Perfectionism can be a major roadblock to progress. The desire to get everything just right, to produce something flawless from the start, can lead to procrastination and inaction. One of the most important lessons I've learned is the value of getting a rough first draft done—of anything, whether it's a project, a piece of writing, or a plan—without waiting too long.

A rough first draft doesn't have to be perfect. In fact, it shouldn't be. The purpose of a first draft is to get your ideas out of your head and into a tangible form. It's a starting point, something you can build on, refine, and improve. But without that first draft, there's nothing to work with.

I used to struggle with this myself. I would spend so much time thinking, planning, and trying to get everything just right in my head before even starting. However, this approach often led to delays, frustration, and missed opportunities. It wasn't until I started forcing myself to get a rough first draft done—no matter how imperfect—that I began to make real progress.

The beauty of a rough first draft is that it frees you from the pressure of perfection. It allows you to experiment, to explore different ideas, and to make mistakes without fear. Once you have something on paper (or on-screen), you can step back, evaluate it, and start the process of revision and improvement.

It's also important to recognize that the first draft is just that—a first draft. It's not the final product, and it doesn't have to be. The process of refining, revising, and polishing comes later, and that's where the real magic happens. But none of that can happen without that initial rough draft.

So, whatever you're working on, don't wait too long to get started. Don't let the fear of imperfection hold you back. Get that rough first draft done, and give yourself something to work with. You'll find that the process of creation becomes much easier, and you'll make far more progress than if you wait for the "perfect" idea or plan to come along.

Chapter 4.8

Don't Be Afraid to Risk It All and Start Over Again

Growing up in Lebanon, I witnessed more than my fair share of hardship. The country I love so dearly has been scarred by wars, conflicts, and instability for the past 30 years. But despite all the destruction, despite the seemingly endless cycle of loss and rebuilding, the people of Lebanon have never lost their spirit, their resilience. They've taught me—and the world—a powerful lesson about what it means to risk everything and start over, again and again, without losing hope.

I remember being a child during the Civil War, the sound of bombs in the distance, the uncertainty that hung in the air like a dark cloud. My family, like so many others, lived with the constant fear that everything we had could be taken away in an instant. And yet, every time the dust settled, my parents and neighbours would go out and begin the work of rebuilding—our homes, our lives, and our communities.

There was something remarkable about the way people picked up the pieces, even when it felt like there were no pieces left to pick up. The war would destroy buildings, take lives, and shatter families, but it never seemed to touch the spirit of the Lebanese people. I saw it in the eyes of my father, who would gather his worn-out tools and set to work repairing our house, time and time again. I saw it in the determination of the shopkeepers who would reopen their businesses, no matter how often they had to start from scratch.

As I grew older, the conflicts continued. There was the war with Israel in 2006 and, more recently, the ongoing turmoil and economic collapse that have plagued the country. Each time, the cycle repeated: destruction, despair, and then, remarkably, hope and rebuilding.

I've seen entire neighbourhoods reduced to rubble, only to be rebuilt with even greater vigour. I've watched as people who have lost everything have found the strength to start over, using whatever they had left. They would gather the few tools they had, even if those tools were worn out and barely functional, and they would begin to rebuild. It wasn't just about restoring what was lost—it was about proving that no matter what happened, they would not be broken.

I carry the resilience of the Lebanese people with me every day. It's a lesson I've taken to heart, especially now that I live in Montreal and face the challenges of life in a new country. Whenever I feel overwhelmed or discouraged, I think back to those days in Lebanon, when it seemed like everything was lost, and yet, somehow, we found the strength to start over.

One of the most important things I've learned is that starting over isn't a sign of failure—it's a testament to our ability to endure. It's about risking everything, knowing that you might lose, but being willing to take that risk anyway. It's about picking up the worn-out tools you have left and using them to rebuild, even when it feels like the odds are stacked against you.

I share this story with my students, hoping they'll understand that life will always present challenges and that there will be times when they'll have to start over. But I also want them to know that they can always rebuild and that they have the strength within them to face any obstacle. It's not about never failing—it's about refusing to be defeated by failure.

Lebanon's history is full of stories of resilience, of people who risked everything and built it all up again, even when it seemed impossible. This history has shaped me and taught me the value of perseverance and the importance of never giving up, no matter how many times you have to start over.

So, whenever I face a new challenge, I remember my

youth's lessons, the Lebanese people's strength, and the unwavering determination to keep going, no matter what. It's a lesson I carry with me and one that I hope to pass on to those around me: Don't be afraid to risk it all and start over again. Because in the end, it's not about how many times you fall—it's about how many times you get back up and keep going. Never be afraid to lose everything. Each morning, I pray and converse with God, reminding myself that I came into this world with nothing and will leave with nothing. I deeply understand that any achievements, rewards, or money are temporary. I keep this awareness in the back of my mind and never let it become the main focus of my life.

I always try to humble myself through experiences, immersing myself in environments where I have nothing. This is why I pilgrimage every year, travelling thousands of kilometres, avoiding comfort and luxury. The strongest people I know are those who are not afraid of losing everything and starting over with renewed drive and purpose.

Chapter 4.9

People & the World: Either Teach and Create – Don't Complain

One of my favourite movies starts with a line narrated by Jack Nicholson: "I don't want to be a product of my environment; I want my environment to be a product of me." This line from "The Departed" left a lasting mark on my life. I always wanted to positively impact the world around me. As I got older, I aimed to leave a hotel room, my neighborhood, and the world in better condition than when I arrived.

You must sacrifice to give back to your community and impact the world. The bigger the sacrifice, the more significant the impact. It's easy to be selfish, live safely, and complain. It's hard to go into the unknown, knowing you may not be adequately compensated for your impact.

Teaching is the most rewarding profession I've witnessed. My mother was a teacher, and I became a teacher and professor, partly to make her proud. Despite teaching at a prestigious university, I often feel underpaid, considering the time and effort required for preparation, presentation, and management. Yet, we continue because nothing is more rewarding than positively impacting younger generations and leaving a lasting mark on the world.

At the beginning of every semester, I question why I teach, but by the end, I pray it never ends. I build relationships with my students that go beyond the classroom. I feel like I have thousands of brothers and sisters worldwide. Teaching allows me to create, make, and work towards a future of happiness and peace, instead of complaining and remaining unhappy.

In a world full of challenges, it's easy to complain. However, complaining rarely leads to productive outcomes. Instead, focusing on teaching and creating yields positive results. Teaching allows you to share knowledge and skills, empowering others and fostering growth. Creating adds value to the world through art, technology, or innovative solutions.

By teaching and creating, you become a proactive force for change, shifting focus from problems to improvements. This mindset encourages positivity and cultivates a sense of purpose and fulfillment.

Chapter 4.10

Listen to People You Don't Get Along With

In school, we're often forced to listen to advice from others, assuming they know more than us. As we grow older, we realize that's not always true. We become more resistant to advice, sometimes viewing it as an insult.

As we age, we narrow our friend groups to those we get along with, avoiding those who challenge us. However, it's worthwhile to listen to people we disagree with, as their insights may save our lives or improve them.

You don't have to agree with everything people say, but you should never stop listening. Listening is crucial for success and is more important now in our polarized world. Whether in politics or personal relationships, listening fosters understanding and prevents violence.

On a less political level, listening helps with careers, relationships, friendships, and love life. Listening to people you don't get along with can be challenging, but it is a crucial step toward personal growth and conflict resolution. These individuals often provide perspectives and insights that you might not encounter otherwise. By actively listening, you can understand their viewpoints, identify common ground, and find ways to bridge gaps.

This practice enhances your ability to navigate diverse opinions and handle disagreements constructively. It fosters open-mindedness and empathy, helping to build more harmonious and collaborative relationships. Additionally, it can lead to unexpected learning opportunities and personal growth as you challenge your assumptions and broaden your understanding of the world.

Let me tell you another story from my teaching experience. Over the years, as a professor in Montreal, I've had the privilege of meeting and working with people from all walks of life. It's one of the things I love most about my job—the diversity of thought, experience, and perspective that my students and colleagues bring into my life. But if there's one lesson that's taken me time to understand fully, it's the importance of listening to people you don't get along with.

Let me tell you about a time when I learned this lesson the hard way.

A few years ago, I had a student in one of my classes called Sam. From the very first day, it was clear that Sam and I didn't see eye to eye. He was outspoken and unafraid to challenge my ideas or how I taught, and our exchanges became heated more than once. I could tell he didn't like me much, and to be honest, I wasn't too fond of him either. He had a way of getting under my skin, of questioning everything I said, which only fueled the tension between us.

For a while, I did what most people do when encountering someone they don't get along with—I avoided him as much as possible. I kept our interactions brief and to the point, and I didn't engage with his challenges any more than I had to. I figured everything would be fine as long as I could get through the semester without too much conflict.

But the thing about Sam was that he wasn't the type to be ignored. He kept pushing and challenging me, and it became clear that he wasn't going to back down. I could either continue to avoid him or confront the issue head-on.

One day, after another tense exchange in class, I decided to do something different. Instead of brushing or shutting him off, I asked Sam to stay after class. I could see the surprise in his eyes—he probably expected me to reprimand him, but that wasn't what I had in mind.

When the classroom was empty, I sat down with him and said, "Sam, I know we don't see things the same way. But I want to understand where you're coming from. Let's talk."

At first, he was hesitant. He wasn't used to me asking for his perspective, and I could tell he wasn't sure if I was being genuine. But slowly, he began to open up. He told me about his experiences, his frustrations with how specific topics were presented in class, and why he felt the need to challenge the status quo.

As I listened, really listened, I began to see things differently. It wasn't that Sam was trying to undermine me—he genuinely cared about the subject, and he had a different perspective that I hadn't considered. His challenges weren't about proving me wrong but seeking a deeper understanding and ensuring that all voices were heard.

That conversation changed everything between Sam and me and how I approached my teaching and interactions with others. I realized that the people we don't get along with often have the most to teach us—if we're willing to listen. It's easy to dismiss someone we don't agree with, to write them off as demanding or argumentative. But when we take the time to listen, we open ourselves up to new ideas, new perspectives, and a deeper understanding of the world around us.

By the end of the semester, Sam and I had developed a mutual respect. We didn't always agree, but that was okay. We both learned from each other, and I'm grateful for the challenges he presented. He made me a better professor, and I'd like to think I helped him see things in a new light.

Now, whenever I encounter someone I don't get along with—a student, a colleague, or someone in my personal life—I remind myself of that experience with Sam. I make a conscious effort to listen, to hear what they're saying, and to understand where they're coming from. It's not always easy, and it doesn't always lead to agreement, but it always leads to growth.

Chapter 4.11

All You Had to Do Is Ask and Aim

A mentor once told me that people rarely say no and are prone to help and support. It's in our nature.

Asking for what you need and setting clear goals are fundamental steps toward achieving your aspirations. Whether it's seeking help, gaining clarity, or pursuing opportunities, asking opens doors that might otherwise remain closed. It demonstrates initiative, builds confidence, and creates pathways for collaboration and support.

Aiming, or setting goals, provides direction and purpose. Clear, well-defined goals help you focus your efforts, measure progress, and stay motivated.

Together, asking and aiming empower you to take control of your journey, actively shaping your path rather than passively reacting to circumstances.

Let me tell you a short story about it.

When I first started my career as a professor in Montreal, I was determined to succeed on my own terms. Like many people, I believed that hard work and determination would be enough to achieve my goals. I was proud of my independence, and I rarely sought help from others, convinced that asking for assistance was a sign of weakness. I believed that if I was capable, I should be able to handle everything on my own.

But there was one experience early in my career that changed my perspective and taught me the power of simply asking—and the importance of aiming for what I truly wanted.

It was my first year at the university, and I was eager to make an impression. I had grand ideas for a research project that I was passionate about, but there was one problem: I needed funding. Without financial support, my project would never get off the ground. I spent weeks working on a proposal, pouring all my energy into crafting a perfect pitch, but the more I worked on it, the more I realized that I lacked the connections and experience to secure the funding I needed.

Despite my growing doubts, I was determined to push through on my own. I kept telling myself that if I just worked harder, I could figure it out. But as the deadline approached, I realized I was running out of time, and I was no closer to securing the support I needed. I was frustrated and anxious, unsure of what to do next.

That's when I remembered something a mentor had once told me: "People rarely say no, especially when you ask for help with sincerity and clarity. It's in our nature to want to help others. All you have to do is ask."

The words stuck with me. Maybe I had been going about this the wrong way. Instead of struggling in silence, maybe I needed to reach out, to ask for the help and guidance I so desperately needed.

With that thought in mind, I decided to do something that felt uncomfortable at first—I asked for help. I reached out to a senior professor in my department, someone I respected but had always been too intimidated to approach. I explained my situation, shared my passion for the project, and asked for his advice on how to secure the funding.

To my surprise, he didn't hesitate. He listened carefully, offered valuable feedback on my proposal, and even suggested a few contacts who might be interested in supporting the project. He didn't see my request as a burden—in fact, he seemed genuinely eager to help. With his guidance, I was able to refine my proposal and connect with the right people. Within a few weeks, I had secured the funding I needed to bring my project to life.

That experience taught me a powerful lesson: asking for help is not a sign of weakness; it's a sign of strength. It takes courage to admit that you don't have all the answers, and it's in those moments of vulnerability that you open yourself up to new possibilities. By asking, I had unlocked doors that would have remained closed if I had tried to go it alone.

But there was another aspect to this experience that was just as important: the idea of aiming. Before I could ask for help, I had to be clear about what I wanted to achieve. I had to set a goal, aim for it, and then take the necessary steps to pursue it. Setting that clear, well-defined goal gave me direction and purpose, and it allowed me to focus my efforts on what truly mattered.

In the years since, I've carried these lessons with me. Whenever I find myself facing a challenge, I remind myself to ask for help when I need it and to always aim for what I truly want. These two principles—asking and aiming—have empowered me to take control of my journey, to shape my path rather than simply reacting to whatever comes my way.

I share this story with my students, hoping to impart the same wisdom that changed my own life. I tell them that it's okay to ask for help, that people are often more willing to assist than we think. And I encourage them to set clear goals, to aim high, and to pursue their aspirations with purpose and determination.

Because in the end, all you really have to do is ask and aim. The rest will follow.

We Make Mistakes, Mistakes Make Us

" Poem

"Lives Within." – by Tarek Riman

In the battle of life, not every win's a prize,
Sometimes the treasure lies in letting go,
In stepping back to see the broader skies,
Where joy resides and softer breezes blow.

Not every fight is worth the sweat and strain,
Not every race demands a winning stride,
For peace can come in moments we refrain,
And find the strength to set our pride aside.

We learn with time that worth's not always proved,
In victories tall or trophies on display,
But in the quiet moments gently moved,
Where love and laughter softly light the way.

So let the need to conquer gently fade,
Embrace the journey, savor every view,
For in the end, it's not the games we've played,
But how we've grown and who we've journeyed to.

And when you find the urge to prove your place,
Remember this: you are enough, right now.
No need to rush or join the frantic race,
Just breathe, be still, and feel the peaceful vow.

For life's true joy is found not in the win,
But in the love and light that lives within.

Chapter 5
You

Summary:

While competition can be motivating, it's important to know when to step back and focus on enjoying the journey rather than always striving to come out on top. This chapter emphasizes that you don't have to win every battle; sometimes, the real victory lies in letting go, collaborating, and finding joy in the experience itself, leading to a more balanced and fulfilling life.

My Mistake: As a middle child, I grew up in a competitive environment and learned that trying to win everything can lead to stress and strained relationships.

Chapter 5.1

You Don't Have to Win Everything

Being the middle child in a family of three boys, everything was competitive.

I always told people that "As a middle child your worth is not given, it has to be made. We had to forge our own way through the world".

I once told a friend that growing up, I had to eat food hot out of the oven because if I didn't, my brothers would eat it. It was the Wild West, or rather the Wild Beirut. No one gave you anything; you had to take it.

Competition was part of the family, whether in games or grades (though I wasn't very competitive academically). Growing up, you realize that trying to win everything can lead to stress and lost friendships. The point of playing a game is to have fun and stay healthy, not to be miserable and stressed.

You don't have to lose your competitive spirit, but you should know when to compete and enjoy life. The desire to win and succeed is a powerful motivator but can also lead to unnecessary stress and conflict. Accepting that you don't have to win every argument or competition is a liberating realization. It allows you to focus on what truly matters and to prioritize your energy and resources effectively.

This mindset encourages collaboration and compromise, fostering healthier relationships and more sustainable outcomes. It helps you to recognize when it is more important to preserve relationships, learn from the experience, or support others' success rather than to win at all costs. Embracing this principle leads to a more balanced and fulfilling life, where the pursuit of personal victories is tempered by empathy, humility, and a broader perspective on success.

Let me tell you a short story.

Growing up as the middle child in a family of three boys, everything in our house was a competition. Whether it was who could run the fastest, jump the highest, or make the best argument at the dinner table, my brothers and I were always trying to outdo each other. As the middle child, I felt like I had to prove myself constantly sandwiched between my older brother, the natural leader, and my younger brother, the charming one. Winning became my way of standing out and ensuring I wasn't overlooked.

This competitive streak followed me well into adulthood. I approached everything with the mindset that if I wasn't winning, I wasn't succeeding. Whether it was sports, work projects, or even friendly games, I always felt this need to come out on top. It wasn't enough to participate; I had to win. But as time passed,

I realized that this constant drive to win was wearing me down, and I wasn't always enjoying the journey.

One day, I had an experience that changed my thoughts about winning.

It was during a casual weekend with my brothers. We had decided to go on a hiking trip, something we used to do as kids. The plan was to climb a mountain trail that we hadn't tackled in years, and as usual, I immediately turned it into a competition in my mind. I was determined to reach the summit first, to prove that I was still as strong and capable as I had always been.

The hike started off well, but as we got deeper into the trail, I noticed something different. My older brother, who usually led the pack, wasn't pushing to be first. Instead, he was walking at a steady pace, stopping often to enjoy the view, to take pictures, and to soak in the experience. My younger brother, usually so energetic and quick, was doing the same—he'd pause to examine a unique rock or point out a bird he hadn't seen before. Meanwhile, I was powering ahead, focused on the goal of reaching the top.

But as I got closer to the summit, I realized something: I wasn't enjoying the hike. I was so focused on winning, on being the first to reach the top, that I was missing out on everything else. I wasn't taking in the beautiful scenery, I wasn't enjoying the company of my brothers, and I wasn't appreciating the moment. All I could think about was getting to the top and winning.

When I finally reached the summit, I stood there alone, looking out at the view. It was stunning, but it felt empty without anyone to share it with. My brothers arrived a few minutes later, laughing and chatting, clearly having enjoyed the hike in a way that I hadn't. They weren't concerned about who had reached the top first; they were happy to have made the journey together.

As we sat at the summit, catching our breath and enjoying the view, I realized that I had missed the point.

The hike wasn't about winning or being the fastest—it was about spending time together, enjoying nature, and creating memories. My brothers had understood this from the start, while I had been caught up in my own need to win.

That day taught me a valuable lesson. Life isn't always about being the best or finishing first. Sometimes, the most meaningful experiences come when you let go of the need to win and simply enjoy the journey. It's about the conversations you have along the way, the moments of laughter, and the shared experiences that make life rich and fulfilling.

Now, I try to approach life differently. Whether it's a project at work, a weekend activity, or even just a simple game, I remind myself that winning isn't everything. It's about being present, appreciating the people around you, and finding joy in the experience itself.

So, when I talk to my students or reflect on my own life, I often think back to that hike. It wasn't the victory of reaching the top that mattered—it was the journey, the time spent with my brothers, and the lesson that you don't have to win everything to enjoy life. Sometimes, the real victory is in letting go and savouring the moment.

Chapter 5.2

Treat Yourself Like You Would Treat a Loved One - Who Are You Putting on a Pedestal?

One of the most profound lessons I've learned is the importance of treating yourself with the same kindness, compassion, and respect that you would offer to a loved one. We often go out of our way to take care of the people we love, to make sure they're happy, healthy, and supported. But when it comes to ourselves, we can be our own worst critics, harshest judges, and most demanding taskmasters.

I used to put everyone else on a pedestal—my friends, my family, my colleagues—believing that their needs, their happiness, and their success were more important than mine. I thought that by putting others first, I was being selfless, noble, and caring. But over time, I realized that this mindset was not only unsustainable but also deeply damaging to my own well-being.

When you constantly put others on a pedestal, you risk losing sight of your own worth, your own needs, and your own happiness. You start to believe that your value is tied to how much you can give, how much you can do for others, and how much you can sacrifice. But this way of thinking is a recipe for burnout, resentment, and a sense of emptiness.

It's important to remember that you are just as deserving of love, care, and compassion as anyone else. You deserve to be treated with kindness, to have your needs met, and to be happy. This doesn't mean that you should stop caring for others or put yourself above everyone else. It simply means that you should include yourself in the circle of people you care for.

One of the ways to start treating yourself like a loved one is to listen to your own needs and desires. What do you need to feel fulfilled, happy, and at peace? What makes you feel loved and appreciated? Take the time to nurture yourself, to do things that bring you joy, and to create a life that supports your well-being.

Another important aspect of treating yourself with kindness is to stop comparing yourself to others. When you put others on a pedestal, you're often comparing their best qualities to your perceived shortcomings. This comparison is not only unfair but also unproductive. Instead, focus on your own strengths, your own achievements, and your own unique journey.

Remember, the relationship you have with yourself is the foundation for all other relationships in your life. If you don't treat yourself with love and respect, it will be difficult to truly love and respect others. By taking care of yourself, by valuing yourself, and by treating yourself with the same kindness you would offer to a loved one, you'll not only improve your own life but also the lives of those around you.

So, take yourself off the pedestal of self-criticism and put yourself on the pedestal of self-love. Treat yourself with the kindness, compassion, and respect that you deserve. You'll find that when you do, everything else in your life begins to fall into place.

Chapter 5.3

How You Treat Yourself

Have you ever noticed that you treat yourself better around others than you do when you're alone? Do you only order certain dishes in the company of others but not when you're by yourself? Do you neglect your health when you get sick, but worry more about others when they do? Have you ever bought a gift for someone that you would never buy for yourself or treated someone to an activity you wouldn't do alone?

Stand in line if you relate to these experiences. Have you ever realized how poorly you treat yourself after someone who cares about you treats you well? Would you ever treat others as badly as you might treat yourself? I answer "yes" to all these questions, and I know many of you will too.

There were times I traveled and slept in the woods or at the door of a monastery to save money and time. Would I do this to someone I love? No, not even to a stranger. So why treat me worse than a stranger?

I lack self-compassion. I won't say everyone does, but I will admit my own struggle. However, I want to tell you, that you are enough and worth it. I say this from experience, having lived a life thinking I wasn't enough or didn't deserve good things.

Now, I'm working on it. I take time off to treat myself, and it feels incredible. I'm slowly becoming addicted to it and wish I could do it more often.

Self-compassion is crucial for well-being and personal growth. Treating yourself with the same kindness, patience, and understanding that you offer loved ones can transform your relationship with yourself. This means being gentle when you make mistakes, celebrating your successes, and caring for your mental and physical health.

Self-compassion fosters resilience, reduces stress, and enhances overall happiness. It allows you to approach challenges with a balanced perspective and maintain a healthier, more positive self-image. By treating yourself like a loved one, you cultivate a nurturing inner dialogue that supports your growth and well-being.

Chapter 5.4

What Is Good for You Is Better Than What You Want

Like most people, when I was younger, I often found myself chasing after the things I wanted. I had dreams, ambitions, and a clear idea of what I thought would make me happy. Whether it was a job, a relationship, or a particular lifestyle, I was determined to get what I wanted, convinced that achieving those desires would bring me fulfillment. But life has a way of teaching you that what you want isn't always what's best for you.

There's one experience that stands out to me, a time when I learned this lesson in a way I'll never forget.

It was during the early years of my career as a professor. I was ambitious, driven, and eager to make a name for myself. I had my sights set on a prestigious position at a well-known university. It was the kind of opportunity that could fast-track my career, open doors, and give me the recognition I craved. I worked tirelessly on my application, polished my resume, and prepared for the interviews with a single-minded focus. I wanted that job more than anything.

When I was finally called in for an interview, I felt confident. I had done everything right, and I believed I was the perfect fit for the position. The interview went well—at least, I thought it did—and I left feeling certain that the job was mine.

But a week later, I received a letter in the mail. It was a polite, formal rejection. They had chosen someone else. I was devastated. All that work, all that effort, and for what? I had been so sure that this job was what I needed to succeed, and now it was slipping through my fingers.

For days, I couldn't shake the disappointment. I kept replaying the interview in my head, wondering what I could have done differently. I wanted that job so badly, and the rejection felt like a personal failure.

But life, as it often does, had other plans for me. Just a few weeks after that rejection, I was offered a position at a different university—not as prestigious, not as well-known, but still a solid opportunity. At first, I was hesitant. It wasn't what I wanted. It wasn't the job I had been dreaming of. But with no other options on the horizon, I decided to take it.

Looking back now, I realize that accepting that job was one of the best decisions I ever made. The university was smaller, but it offered me opportunities I never would have had at the prestigious institution. I was given the freedom to explore my own research interests, to develop new courses, and to work closely with students in a way that was deeply fulfilling. The community was supportive, the environment was collaborative, and I found myself growing both professionally and personally in ways I hadn't expected.

Over time, I came to understand that what I thought I wanted—the prestigious job, the recognition, the fast-track career—wasn't what I really needed. What was good for me, what truly brought me happiness and fulfillment, was something different entirely. It was the opportunity to grow, to learn, and to make a meaningful impact in a place where I could be myself.

That experience taught me an invaluable lesson: what is good for you is often better than what you want. We can get so caught up in our desires, in the things we think will make us happy, that we lose sight of what's really important. But life has a way of guiding us toward what we truly need, even if it's not what we originally had in mind.

Now, when I face decisions or when things don't go as planned, I remind myself of that time in my life. I remind myself that sometimes, what we want isn't what's best for us, and that there's wisdom in trusting the journey, in being open to the unexpected opportunities that come our way.

I share this story with my students, encouraging them to keep an open mind and to trust that life often knows better than we do. It's not always easy to let go of our desires, but when we do, we might just find that what we receive in return is far greater than anything we could have imagined.

So, whenever I think about that job I didn't get, I smile. Because in the end, not getting what I wanted turned out to be the best thing that could have happened to me. It led me to where I was meant to be, and it taught me that what is good for you is always better than what you think you want.

Desires and wants often stem from immediate gratification or external influences, while what is genuinely good for you aligns with your long-term well-being and deeper values. Understanding this difference icial for making decisions that lead to lasting fulfillment.

Prioritizing what is good for you over what you want may involve sacrifices or delayed gratification, but it ultimately leads to more meaningful and sustainable outcomes. This principle encourages you to focus on long-term benefits and personal growth, guiding you toward choices that nurture your overall health and happiness.

Chapter 5.5

Stop Trying to Prove Yourself

Constantly trying to prove yourself can be exhausting and counterproductive. It often stems from external pressures and a desire for validation, leading to stress and diminished self-worth. Instead of seeking external approval, focus on your intrinsic value and personal goals.

Recognize that you are enough as you are, and that your worth is not contingent on external achievements or validation. This shift in mindset allows you to pursue your passions and goals for their own sake, fostering a more authentic and fulfilling life. By letting go of the need to prove yourself, you free up energy to invest in what truly matters, leading to greater contentment and self-acceptance..

Here is a short story.

Back to growing up as the middle child in a family of three boys, I always felt like I was in the middle of a constant struggle to prove myself. There was, in between, trying to carve out my own identity to show that I was just as capable and worthy of recognition.

That need to prove myself followed me into adulthood. I poured myself into my work, determined to stand out. Over the years, I wrote books, built a business, and took on challenges that pushed me to my limits. I was driven by this underlying belief that I needed to achieve more, to keep proving that I wasn't just the middle child, but someone who could make a real impact.

But no matter how much I accomplished, there was always a part of me that felt it wasn't enough. I kept setting higher goals, pushing myself harder, always looking for that next achievement that would finally make me feel like I had proven my worth.

One day, after finishing a particularly challenging project, I sat down and started reflecting on why I was pushing myself so hard. I had achieved many of the things I'd set out to do, but I still felt this pressure to keep going, to do more. It was then that I realized I wasn't just driven by passion or ambition; I was driven by the need to prove myself and seek validation from others.

That realization was eye-opening. I started to see that no matter how much I achieved, it would never feel like enough if I was always looking for external validation. I had to learn to recognize my own worth, not because of what I had accomplished, but because of who I was. I didn't need to keep competing or pushing myself to prove something. I was enough, just as I was.

Letting go of that constant need to prove myself wasn't easy, but it was liberating. I began to approach my work with a renewed sense of purpose, focusing on what truly mattered to me rather than on what I thought would earn me recognition. I found more joy in the process, more fulfillment in the journey, and a deeper sense of peace in knowing that I didn't need to prove anything to anyone.

Looking back, I realize that success isn't about proving yourself to others or even to yourself. It's about being true to who you are, pursuing what you love, and finding contentment in the process. Being the middle child taught me many lessons, but the most important one was that I didn't need to prove myself to be worthy. I just needed to be myself, and that was enough.

Chapter 5.6

Talent Alone

In the pursuit of success, it's easy to fall into the trap of believing that talent is the ultimate key to achieving greatness. From a young age, we're often told stories of prodigies—those individuals who seem to effortlessly excel in their chosen fields, whether in music, sports, academics, or the arts. These stories create the impression that talent is a magical ingredient, the secret sauce that sets the extraordinary apart from the ordinary.

However, as we dig deeper into the lives of those who have achieved true greatness, a different picture emerges. Talent, while certainly valuable, is not the be-all and end-all of success. In fact, research and countless real-life examples suggest that something else plays a far more critical role: grit.

Grit, as defined by psychologist Angela Duckworth, is the combination of passion and perseverance. It's the quality that keeps people going when the going gets tough, the drive that pushes them to continue practicing, learning, and improving long after the initial excitement has worn off. Grit is what turns talent into skill and skill into achievement. It's the relentless pursuit of a goal, even in the face of obstacles, setbacks, and failures.

Here is a story from one of my classes.

There was a student I once knew named Emily, who was known for her remarkable talent in writing. From a young age, she had a way with words that left her teachers and peers in awe. Her essays were often used as examples in class, and she frequently won writing competitions without seeming to put in much effort. It was clear to everyone around her that Emily had a gift, and many expected that she would go on to achieve great things as a writer.

But as Emily grew older and moved on to higher levels of education, something began to change. The assignments became more challenging, the competition more intense. While she still had that natural talent, she started to struggle. She found herself facing deadlines she couldn't meet, and the effortless flow of words she had once known began to falter. For the first time in her life, Emily's talent didn't seem to be enough.

At first, she was frustrated and confused. She had always been told how talented she was, how writing came so naturally to her. But now, she felt like she was losing her touch. She started to doubt herself, wondering if maybe she wasn't as good as everyone had always said. The pressure to live up to the expectations of others—and of herself—was overwhelming.

During this time, Emily began to notice another student in her class, a girl named Sarah. Sarah wasn't known for her talent in writing. In fact, she had struggled with it for as long as anyone could remember. But what Sarah lacked in natural ability, she made up for in something else entirely: grit. Sarah worked tirelessly on her assignments, revising drafts over and over, seeking feedback, and never giving up, even when her work was criticized or when she received lower grades than she had hoped for.

Emily watched as Sarah slowly but surely improved, each piece of writing better than the last. While Emily was caught up in her frustration and doubt, Sarah kept moving forward, undeterred by setbacks. It was clear that Sarah didn't have the same natural talent, but she had something else—an unyielding determination to succeed, no matter how difficult the journey.

One day, after receiving a particularly disappointing grade, Emily decided to talk to Sarah. She was curious about how Sarah managed to keep going, even when things didn't come easily to her. Sarah's response was simple but profound: "I know I'm not the best writer, but I love it, and I want to get better. I've learned that talent can only take you so far. What really matters is how hard you're willing to work."

That conversation struck a chord with Emily. She realized that she had been relying too much on her natural talent and not enough on the hard work and perseverance that true success requires. She had been coasting on her abilities, but now she saw that talent alone wasn't enough to carry her through the challenges she was facing.

Inspired by Sarah's determination, Emily decided to change her approach. She started to put in the work, revising her drafts multiple times, seeking feedback from her teachers, and embracing the challenges instead of shying away from them. It wasn't easy—there were still moments of frustration and doubt—but Emily was determined to improve, to push herself beyond the limits of her natural talent.

Over time, Emily began to see the results of her efforts. Her writing became more refined, more powerful. She started to regain her confidence, not because of her talent, but because of the hard work she was putting in. She learned that success wasn't just about being naturally gifted—it was about having the grit to keep going, to keep improving, and to never give up, no matter how tough things got.

By the end of the school year, Emily had grown not just as a writer, but as a person. She no longer saw herself as just a talented writer, but as someone who was willing to put in the work to achieve her goals. And in that process, she found a deeper sense of fulfillment and pride in her accomplishments than she ever had when she was relying solely on her talent.

Emily's story is a reminder that while talent can give you a head start, it's grit—passion, perseverance, and hard work—that truly determines how far you'll go. Talent may be the spark that ignites the fire, but it's the consistent effort and determination that keep the flame burning bright.

Chapter 5.7

Find Meaning

I've lived through my share of tough times, moments that tested my strength and resilience in ways I never anticipated. Growing up, there were days when the world felt like it was crumbling around me. I remember the hours spent in bomb shelters during times of conflict, the tension and fear hanging in the air, the uncertainty of what the next day—or even the next hour—would bring. In those dark moments, it was easy to feel lost, to wonder what the point of it all was. But through it all, I discovered something powerful: finding meaning in life is essential for enduring suffering and achieving fulfillment.

Life is full of challenges—relationship struggles, work problems, moments of deep unfairness. Each one of these trials can feel like a heavy weight, pulling us down, making us question our path. But when we find meaning and purpose in what we do, it becomes easier to navigate through those difficult times. Purpose gives us a reason to keep going, to push through the pain, and to emerge stronger on the other side.

For me, finding that meaning didn't come all at once. It was a gradual process, shaped by experiences and the people I met along the way. I learned that purpose isn't something that magically appears; it's something you build, piece by piece, through your actions, your values, and your connections with others. And once you have it, it acts as a guiding light, helping you find your way out of even the darkest corners.

But there's another layer to this journey of finding meaning, and it has to do with how we view ourselves and our potential. This is where the concept of a growth mindset comes into play. For a long time, I believed that our abilities were fixed—that we were born with a certain level of talent or intelligence, and that was that. But as I encountered more challenges, I began to see things differently.

The idea of a growth mindset, which I came across in my reading and conversations, transformed the way I approached life. Instead of seeing setbacks as failures, I started to view them as opportunities to learn and grow. I realized that our abilities aren't set in stone; they can be developed and expanded through effort, perseverance, and the right mindset.

This shift in perspective changed everything for me. It made me more resilient in the face of adversity, more willing to take risks, and more open to new experiences. I stopped fearing failure and started embracing it as a natural part of the growth process. And with each challenge I faced, I found that I was not only getting better at what I did, but I was also finding deeper meaning and fulfillment in my life.

Success and personal development are deeply intertwined with our beliefs about our abilities. When we embrace a growth mindset, we open ourselves up to a world of possibilities. We become more adaptable, more creative, and more persistent. And in doing so, we unlock the potential for greater accomplishments and a more fulfilling life.

So, as I reflect on those tough moments—whether it was in a bomb shelter, dealing with personal or professional challenges, or facing the unfairness of the world—I see them now as part of a larger journey. A journey where finding meaning and embracing a growth mindset have helped me not only to endure but to thrive.

Life will always have its share of hardships, but when we find purpose and believe in our ability to grow, we equip ourselves with the tools to overcome anything. We become, in essence, always growing, always changing, and always finding new ways to achieve fulfillment, no matter what life throws our way.

Chapter 5.8

What Bothers You Now Won't Bother You in the Future

Many of the worries and anxieties that consume us today lose their significance over time. The issues that seem insurmountable now often fade in importance as circumstances change and we grow. Understanding this can provide a sense of perspective and reduce the weight of current concerns. By focusing on long-term goals and maintaining a forward-looking mindset, you can better navigate present challenges with the assurance that they will likely diminish in the future.

I am writing this part of the book while in the middle of a course at a major university in Canada. One student complained that the leaderboard was too competitive and overwhelming. I use leaderboards because I love it when students participate. An active class is a learning class. But not everyone agrees with me. The complaint saddened and disappointed me, akin to someone shouting that a game is rigged because they're losing.

I was born and raised in a world where everything is unfair. That's life. You don't complain; you do your best with what you have. That is how civilization is built. If I said this situation doesn't bother me, I'd be lying. It does bother me, but I know that in a few days, I won't even think about it, and in a few years, I will laugh at it.

Believe it or not, when I asked my friends what they thought, I asked them two questions:

- What did I miss?

- What can I learn moving forward?

I was less worried about the situation and more concerned about what I could learn from it.

Play It Out

Visualizing the potential outcomes of your actions and attitudes can be a powerful motivator for change. Consider where your current path might lead you if left unchecked.

Chapter 5.9

If You Are 35 Now and Cynical and Angry, in 10 Years, It Will Be 10 Times Worse

Time changes everything, and what you do with time matters. What you do today will impact your tomorrow. I've seen it happen as I grew up. Spend too much time on your phone or Instagram, and you'll realize that the whole world is passing you by. Spend too much time working, and you'll miss out on your physical health and social life. Time matters, not money.

As I always tell my students, if you are 25 and unsure about your future, you're fine. But by 30, if you're still unsure, it's different. When you're young, you're full of potential. As you get older, you should have more achievements and experience. It's no longer cute to be unsure at 40; you need to be steady.

I tell this to my friends when they're going through tough times, especially if these tough times are lasting longer than they should. If they're miserable in their mid-30s and not doing anything about it, they will be miserable in their mid-40s.

There's a Chinese saying, "The best time to plant a tree was 20 years ago. The second best time is today." There is no better time to be less cynical and take action to improve your life, whether you see the results now or later.

A trick I learned from my business and life coach, Melissa Dawn, is to ask yourself, "What would you 10 years from now do if he were in your shoes right now?" This question has helped me solve many problems and make decisions that impact my life now and in the future.

So I bring it back to you: if you are 30 years old today, what would 40-year-old you want you to do to make his life and your life better now? The answers to this question might surprise you and even change your life.

People joke about "What would Jesus do?" but for me, it's not a joke. I don't like joking about religious things, especially not about Jesus or God. Putting yourself in Jesus's shoes and making decisions based on what he would have done gives you a better perspective on your situation and makes you more forgiving of yourself and others. Forgiveness is one of the strongest messages we've learned from Jesus.

When you ask, "What would Jesus do?" you're asking what one of the most impactful, loving, caring, and forgiving humans would have done. Negative emotions are things we carry, and negativity, over time, intensifies and feels heavier, leading to much more pain.

Negative emotions, if not addressed, can intensify over time, leading to deeper dissatisfaction and unhappiness. If you find yourself harbouring cynicism and anger at 35, these feelings will likely compound if you don't take steps to address them. Without intervention, this path can lead to a more entrenched and pervasive state of negativity, affecting your overall well-being and relationships.

Chapter 5.10

You Have to Change Your Ways, or You Will Go Down a Dreadful Path

Have you ever arrived at a point in time or in a situation and paused to ask yourself, "How the **** did I end up here?" I have. Most of the time, we are the reason we are where we are. I can confidently say this, especially if you're an adult. Yes, you might be born in the wrong country or have a tough childhood, and the odds might not be in your favor early on in life. Yes, you might be a middle child and have physical disadvantages. I check all these boxes and still say life results from my actions. There's no one out there to blame for my shortcomings.

You have to change your ways or go down a dark, dreadful path. The only person who will suffer is you, and the only person to blame is you. I found it dangerous that, at one point in my life, I was on a dreadful path but didn't see the need to change until things got really bad, and I had no choice.

My philosophy teacher used to talk about the "car versus walk decision." If something is one kilometer away, you might consider walking or taking a car. If it's three kilometers away, you might still consider walking or taking a car. But if it's 20 kilometers away, you wouldn't even think about walking. That's how life works sometimes. We need to understand and know when we need to change.

Conversations about this are ones I constantly have with my students and friends. Whenever they are in a tough spot, I ask them, "What are you willing to change, and how far are you willing to go to avoid being in the same situation again?" The most important question is, "Are you willing to change to avoid this happening in the future?"

Recognizing the need for change is the first step toward a more positive future. Acknowledging that continuing down a path of negativity will only worsen your situation can motivate you to seek healthier habits and attitudes. Change might require self-reflection, seeking help, and making conscious efforts to adopt a more positive outlook on life.

We Make Mistakes, Mistakes Make Us

" Poem

"Me and you" – by Tarek Riman

In the heart of war's cruel night,
Where bombs do fall and fear takes flight,
I saw a truth that cuts through strife,
That people, at their core, hold life.

In darkest hours, when hope seems thin,
It's not the bombs that win within,
But hands that reach, and voices kind,
A spark of good in hearts we find.

Strangers in a bunker, bound,
By whispered fears, by common ground,
Yet there in shadowed, trembling air,
A light of love, we all did share.

For though the world outside may burn,
To basic good, we all return,
To comfort, hold, and help each other,
In strangers' arms, we find a brother.

And on the Camino's winding path,
Where pilgrims tread through nature's wrath,
I learned again what I had known,
That kindness makes the journey home.

A German woman, with water spare,
Gave all she had, without a care,
A Jewish friend who shared her bread,
And filled with hope, where fear had led.

A Spanish man who took the strain,
And pushed my bike through mountain's pain,
These acts of grace, they warmed my heart,
Reminding me we're not apart.

For in this life, we walk as one,
Beneath the same, unyielding sun,
No creed, no race, no wall divides,
Just fellow travelers on these tides.

And family, with all its flaws,
Its passive stings, its silent wars,
Yet still, the ties that bind us tight,
Through all the pain, through all the night.

When I returned, my book in hand,
To share the tales of distant land,
Their words were sharp, their praise was thin,
But still, I let their voices in.

For family, with all its ways,
Is love that lasts through all our days,
So call them, hold them, keep them near,
For in their hearts, we find what's dear.

In every act of love we show,
In every seed of good we sow,
We find the truth that life can give,
That in each other, we truly live.

So cherish those who share your days,
In family's light, in strangers' gaze,
For at the end, when all is through,
What matters most is me and you.

Chapter 6
People & Family

Summary:

These chapters explore the inherent goodness in people and the power of human connection. I reflect on a childhood memory of strangers comforting one another in a war-torn bunker, which reaffirmed my belief that people are fundamentally good, especially in the darkest times. This theme continues on the Camino de Santiago, where I experienced profound acts of kindness from fellow pilgrims, highlighting the universal human instinct to help one another regardless of our differences. Finally, in the chapter on family, I emphasize the importance of maintaining relationships with loved ones, despite their flaws, and urge us all to prioritize meaningful connections in our lives.

My Mistake: Sometimes I fail to see the good in people and family, but the reality is that all we have is each other.

Chapter 6.1

People are good.

People are good by nature. Sometimes, situations corrupt us, but in the darkest hours, we stand together.

As I write this on a plane, the guy in front of me is in full recline, while I am trying to work, yet this situation nor any situation should redefine our view of humanity.

I remember one night in Lebanon, when I was a child, we found ourselves huddled in a bunker. The war was raging outside, and the sound of bombs falling from the sky was something I will never forget. The whistling noise of the bombs as they plummeted from an F-16 was one of the most terrifying sounds I had ever heard. It would start with a high-pitched scream, then a whistle, and finally, the ground would shake as the bomb hit its target, shattering windows and sending vibrations through the earth.

That night, the darkness in the bunker was almost absolute. We were a group of strangers thrown together by the circumstances of war. There were no lights, no way to see each other's faces. We were just voices in the dark, breathing heavily, our hearts pounding in unison as we waited for the next bomb to drop. As a child, I was terrified, unsure if we would make it through the night.

But something remarkable happened in that darkness. Despite the fear and the uncertainty, people began to reach out to one another. I remember feeling a hand on my shoulder, a stranger's voice asking if I was okay. I could hear others whispering words of comfort, reassuring each other that we would survive the night, that the bombing would eventually stop, and that the sun would rise again.

In that moment, I realized something profound about human nature. We were all strangers, yet in that bunker, in the darkest hours, we became something more. We became a community, a small group of people bound together by our shared fear and our shared hope. The war outside was a reminder of the worst of humanity, but inside that bunker, in the pitch black, I witnessed the best of it.

The military complex could take away our homes, our safety, even our sense of security, but it couldn't take away our humanity. When everything else was stripped away, what remained was a basic human instinct to care for one another, to hold on to each other in the face of fear and uncertainty. In those moments, people's true nature shone through, and I learned that, at our core, people are good.

As I sit here now, writing this on a plane, I'm reminded of that night in the bunker. The man in front of me has his seat fully reclined, leaving me with little room to move. It's a small inconvenience, something that might normally irritate me, but it doesn't change my view of humanity. The truth is, in our everyday lives, we often focus on the small annoyances, the minor grievances, and we let them color our perception of others.

But when I think back to that night in the bunker, I'm reminded of something much more important. In the darkest moments, when everything else is stripped away, people reveal who they truly are. And more often than not, what I've seen is that people stand together. They reach out, they comfort, they protect one another. We're not defined by the small irritations of everyday life, but by how we respond in the face of true adversity.

War showed me the worst of what humans are capable of, but it also showed me the best. It taught me that understanding people isn't about focusing on their flaws or the small inconveniences they cause. It's about recognizing the fundamental goodness that lies within each of us, the instinct to care for one another, to support each other when it matters most.

So, when I find myself frustrated by something small, like a reclining seat on a plane, I try to remember that night in the bunker. I try to remember the hands reaching out in the dark, the voices whispering words of comfort, and the humanity that shone through in the darkest hour. Because that's who people really are, and that's what I choose to believe in.

Chapter 6.2

Helping each other

As I mentioned throughout the book, I go on a pilgrimage almost every year, the Camino de Santiago.

The Camino is a secular pilgrimage frequented by people of all faiths, including those with no religious beliefs. On my journeys, I have met people of all genders, ages, sexualities and abilities. The Camino is for anyone and everyone. It has no religion, no gender, no color, no bigotry, no misogyny, no racism. It is a human journey for all who want to do it. Some of the most common reactions among those who have done it are, "The Camino changes you", "You're not the same at the end of the Camino as when you started," or "The Camino helps you know yourself."

I didn't come to find God. I came to find myself. I travelled inwards while also conquering raw outdoor spaces.

The Camino is a human experience where we are all walking together and helping each other along the way.

I saw people carrying each other's' bags, some getting bananas for each other, some carrying each other.

Lina Nahhas is a Palestinian-Canadian woman and founder of the Sameness Project who coined the term 'sameness moment'. As she describes it, The Sameness Moment is when you look into the eyes of another human being, and all preconceived notions about culture and identity melt away so you see them as they truly are.

This explains beautifully what it felt like to be a pilgrim among pilgrims. I saw people helping each other all the time. People would go out of their way to help complete strangers. I saw some carrying others when they were too tired or broken to keep going on their own, sharing their last banana or going out of their way to find water for others.

It didn't matter what we were - Catholic or Protestant, Muslim or Jewish, man or woman, gay or straight - there was no division, there was no we/they, no rich/poor. There was only one thing: we are all human on a human journey together. People were lifting one another up, all the time.

The following is a short story of help on my Camino.

The German Woman

I chose to go on a part of the trip that most pilgrims skip: the road between Burgos and Leon. As there is not much to do along this route, I wasn't stopping for many breaks. At one point, I ran out of water. I had biked for 4 hours straight and reached a part where there were 35 KM left till the next stop. I was getting dehydrated and needed water. I even considered drinking from a puddle on the road, but I kept it together, talking myself into being okay. I paced myself and kept moving, trying to expend as little energy as possible.

The last 10 km had me worried. I was lightheaded and felt like passing out. Out of nowhere, I saw a woman looking around. I stopped and asked her for water. She gave me a bottle and I guzzled it down without thinking until I realized there were only a few sips left. I asked her if it was ok to finish it and she said yes.

I finished the water and thanked her, gave her a hug and asked her if she wanted company for the next 7 km. We walked all the way there together.

I learned all about her and the reason she was walking. She waited until we reached the hostel and then ran to the water, as I did. That is when I realized that she had given me all she had. I felt so blessed and, for that brief moment, I had so much hope for humanity.

The Jewish American Woman

I'm a proud Canadian, but as I mentioned, my origins are Lebanese. Growing up in Lebanon, you don't hear much about Jewish people. When I moved to Montreal, I had my first bagel, I ate smoked meat and I made friends with Jewish people. I owe a lot of opportunities in my life and career to my Jewish friends. Sameness. The more I mingled with these people I had been discouraged from mingling with, the more I understood that we shared the same hopes, dreams and aspirations. Even the same worries and concerns.

I met a Jewish woman from the US on one of my Camino journeys. She was so friendly and we enjoyed each other's company so much that I decided to stay behind an extra day with her.

Halfway through the day, I started to feel sick and realized I hadn't eaten since the day before. She gave me some of her food to eat. It was a cheese sandwich and only after I finished eating did I realize it was all the food she had. I never got to thank her, but I'll never forget the kind gesture and great company. It was because of her selflessness that I was able to finish my journey.

The next time you catch yourself falling into ingrained beliefs or stereotypes about any group of people, think twice about it. Ask yourself where your beliefs really come from. Share a meal with that person you think you know so much about. You don't know anything about anyone until you have a conversation with them. Drink some water, break some bread, communicate and that should open your mind. Otherwise, keep your opinions to yourself.

The Spanish Guy

On day 10 of this trip, I was approaching O Cebrero, 1500 meters above sea level, in the province of Castilla y Leon. I ran into a guy who seemed to be quite the athlete. At that point on the mountain, I was unable to continue biking. I had to get off and push my bike up. The guy came over and offered to help push my bike. I looked at him, unaccustomed to having a stranger offer help out of nowhere. I almost asked him why, but then, I really did need help.

Now there are two things that surprised me about this moment. The first was how this guy knew that I really did need help. The second was how utterly selfless his move was.

After living in North American cities, you do get to be more hesitant about trusting just anyone with valuable possessions.

But, this wasn't North America, and this guy wasn't just anyone. He was a fellow pilgrim.

After almost 30 minutes of him pushing my bike uphill, I asked if I could take over. To my third surprise, he replied, "No, you have done enough. You look tired. I will push your bike to the top."

We arrived at the top of the mountain, went to a restaurant and I even had to argue with him to at least let me pay for his meal.

I'm much more accustomed to people turning away when they see a homeless person on the street corner or someone who needs help. People who don't hold doors open for others or give up their subway seat for the elderly. I'm used to people being so self-absorbed that they have no idea what a difference they can make with even the smallest act of kindness. And, after working in the competitive world of marketing agencies, I've been on the receiving end of backstabbing and betrayal, where people will do anything to get ahead.

But there is so much more to be gained through simple acts of kindness.

As I age, I gain more experience in life. There is no better cause to live and die for than helping others.

I tell this to my students all the time: the main purpose we are here is to be angels in each other's lives, to help each other through this crazy journey we call life,

Chapter 6.3

Understand Family

I was born and raised in Lebanon, in the Middle East, in the mountains, on a farm far from civilization. I was born at the end of a 15-year civil war and witnessed several wars throughout my life. Yet, the most violent thing I've seen is the passive aggressiveness of my family, especially when I achieve something meaningful.

When I published my first book, I returned to Lebanon for a fundraiser. We raised a few thousand dollars for scholarships, sold a few hundred books, and made my parents proud. However, it was never easy. I had to face my past failures and talk about them. There were mental, emotional, and physical struggles, including the challenge of using public transport in Lebanon.

After the fundraiser, my book became an international bestseller. I visited my aunts and uncle to give them a copy. The book was about the Camino de Santiago, a 900-kilometer pilgrimage in northern Spain. It was a journey of purity, suffering, love, friendship, connection, gratitude, and perspective. It was life-changing for me, and I hoped my family would find similar inspiration.

However, my uncle's response was, "The pictures are in black and white; not very engaging." My aunt said, "Not enough pictures; I won't read it." They asked for a quick summary, and as I began, they interrupted with their own stories of suffering. I realized they might not be the best audience for my book, so I respectfully excused myself.

Despite their reactions, I love my family. Many of you can relate to this, and we all have similar family issues. We must always check in on our family, put our egos aside, and remember that whatever they say comes from their perspective, not ours.

At the end of every class, I tell my students to call their parents and loved ones. I lost all my grandparents and wish I had called them more often. It's too late for me, but I hope it's not too late for you. Call your family and let them know you love them.

In the fast-paced rhythm of modern life, personal connections often take a backseat. Asking about someone's family is a simple yet powerful gesture that shows genuine interest and care. It acknowledges the importance of family in people's lives and helps build deeper, more meaningful relationships.

Inquiring about family strengthens bonds and provides insights into others' values and priorities. It fosters empathy and understanding, creating a supportive and inclusive environment. This practice can significantly enhance both personal and professional relationships, promoting a culture of respect and connectedness.

We Make Mistakes, Mistakes Make Us

" Poem

"I clipped my wings"– by Tarek Riman

In golden cages, we often dwell,
Protecting our hearts in a guarded shell,
We build these walls, so safe, so high,
Afraid to fail, afraid to try.

From childhood days, I learned the art,
To shield my mind, to guard my heart,
In a family where strength was king,
I wore my armor, tight as string.

Through life's great maze, I kept it close,
Protecting myself from every dose,
Of hurt, of pain, of failure's sting,
I thought I was safe, but I clipped my wings.

The castles we build, so grand, so bright,
With treasures gleaming in the night,
Are prisons masked in gold and sheen,
Where freedom fades and dreams grow lean.

David, my friend, with wealth in hand,
Built a life so safe, so grand,
But in his castle, shining bright,
He found no peace, no sleep at night.

The car that shone with polished grace,
Needed care in every space,

We Make Mistakes, Mistakes Make Us

The house so grand, the gadgets new,
Demanded more than he ever knew.

But as we cling to all we own,
The weight we carry only grows,
For every object, each golden thing,
Becomes a burden, a heavy ring.

In time, I learned, and so did he,
That what we own should set us free,
Not chain us down, or hold us tight,
But let us live in simple light.

So, I let go of the need to shield,
Embraced the wounds that life could yield,
In failing to protect, I found my flight,
In vulnerability, I found my might.

Minimalism, a life of less,
Where every choice brings happiness,
Decluttered spaces, minds at peace,
In less, we find our sweet release.

The towel I carried for miles and miles,
Grew heavy with each passing trial,
But when I let go, the weight did fall,
And I stood up straight, and felt so tall.

For it's not the things that make us whole,
But the freedom to live, to love, to stroll,
Through life's rich path, with lightened feet,
Where less is more, and life is sweet.

True freedom lies in risks we take,
In hearts we trust, in fears we break,
For in the end, it's plain to see,
That in letting go, we set ourselves free.

Chapter 7
Set yourself free

Summary:

These chapters explore the idea that overprotecting ourselves can limit our freedom, using my own experiences to illustrate the point. I learned that excessive self-protection, whether in childhood or while running my business, kept me from fully living and growing. I found true freedom and fulfillment by embracing vulnerability and letting go of control. Similarly, I share the story of my friend David, who built a life of luxury that ultimately became a burden, showing that the pursuit of comfort can trap us if we aren't careful. Lastly, I emphasize the value of minimalism, explaining how simplifying our lives by reducing possessions can lead to greater clarity, freedom, and happiness.

My Mistake: Due to past mistakes, hurts, scarcities and traumas, I always aim to overprotect myself and try to control everything, but as you already know, that is not sustainable.

Chapter 7.1

Fail to Protect Yourself, and You Will Set Yourself Free - Protection Is the Enemy of Freedom

While it's natural to seek safety and security, excessive self-protection can become restrictive. Overprotecting yourself can lead to missed opportunities, stifled growth, and a life constrained by fear. True freedom comes from embracing vulnerability and taking risks. By stepping out of your comfort zone and facing uncertainties, you can discover new possibilities and experiences that enrich your life.

Here is a tough life lesson.

Growing up as the middle child in a family of three boys, I quickly learned how to protect myself—both emotionally and physically. My older brother was stronger, always taking the lead, while my younger brother had a knack for getting away with things, leaving me to fend for myself in the middle. I built up walls, perfected the art of self-defence, and learned to navigate the tricky dynamics of sibling rivalry with care. It became second nature to protect myself, to shield my emotions, and to guard my vulnerabilities.

As I moved into adulthood, that instinct to protect myself didn't just disappear; it became even more ingrained. I approached life with caution, always careful not to expose too much of myself, always ensuring that I stayed in control. Whether it was in relationships, career decisions, or personal aspirations, I made sure that I didn't take unnecessary risks, that I kept a part of myself safely tucked away where no one could reach it. I believed that by protecting myself, I was maintaining control over my life, keeping myself safe from disappointment, failure, and hurt.

But over time, I began to realize that this constant need for protection was also holding me back. The walls I had built to keep myself safe were also keeping me isolated, preventing me from fully experiencing life. I was so focused on guarding myself that I wasn't truly living. I was missing out on opportunities, on connections, on the kind of freedom that comes from letting go of control and allowing yourself to be vulnerable.

The turning point came during a particularly challenging period in my life. I had started my own marketing agency, Riman Agency, and while it was successful, I was constantly stressed, constantly trying to protect the business from any potential failure. I micromanaged every aspect, worried over every decision, and found myself growing increasingly exhausted. The more I tried to protect the agency, the more trapped I felt.

One day, after yet another sleepless night, I had a moment of clarity. I realized that my need for control, my obsession with protecting myself and my business from any possible harm, was suffocating me. I wasn't free—I was trapped by my own fears. I had built a cage around myself, thinking it would keep me safe, but all it had done was limit my ability to grow, to take risks, to truly live.

It was then that I decided to let go. I stopped trying to protect every little thing, stopped worrying about potential failures, and started embracing the idea that vulnerability wasn't a weakness, but a strength. I began to trust my instincts more, to delegate tasks, to take risks without being paralyzed by the fear of failure. I allowed myself to be open to new experiences, even if it meant risking disappointment or hurt.

And something incredible happened: I felt free. The more I let go of the need to protect myself, the more alive I felt. I started to enjoy my work again, to connect more deeply with the people around me, and to find joy in the uncertainties of life. By failing to protect myself, by allowing myself to be vulnerable, I had set myself free.

Looking back, I see now that protection can be the enemy of freedom. When we build walls around ourselves, we may feel safe, but we also limit our ability to experience life fully. True freedom comes from letting go of the need to control everything, from embracing the risks and uncertainties that come with being human. It's about understanding that vulnerability isn't something to fear—it's something that can lead to growth, connection, and a deeper sense of fulfillment.

So now, I remind myself that I don't need to protect myself from every potential hurt or failure. Instead, I focus on living openly, embracing the challenges and joys that come my way, and trusting that by letting go, I am setting myself free.

Chapter 7.2

We Build Golden Castles to Live In, They Become Our Prison

I once had a friend named David who seemed to have it all. He was driven by the desire to create a life that was not only successful but also filled with every comfort money could buy. From the outside, it looked like he was living the dream—a beautiful home, a luxury car, the latest gadgets, and a wardrobe filled with designer clothes. He had crafted what he often referred to as his "golden castle," a life where everything was polished, perfect, and secure.

David's pursuit of comfort and security was relentless. He worked hard, earned well, and spent lavishly, convinced that each new purchase would bring him closer to happiness. Whether it was the latest technology, high-end furniture, or exotic vacations, David believed that surrounding himself with the best would shield him from the uncertainties of life. He wanted a life where everything was in its place, where he would want for nothing, and where his golden castle would be a refuge from the world.

But over time, something began to shift. The more David accumulated, the more he started to feel weighed down. What had once been symbols of success and comfort began to feel like burdens. The luxury car required constant maintenance, the beautiful home demanded endless upkeep, and the gadgets that once excited him quickly became outdated and were replaced by newer, more expensive versions. The things he had bought to enhance his life began to take over it, demanding more of his time, attention, and energy.

The golden castle David had built started to feel less like a haven and more like a trap. He confided in me one evening, admitting that the endless cycle of buying and maintaining was exhausting him. "I thought these things would make me happy," he said, "but now it feels like they own me instead. I'm constantly worried about keeping everything in perfect condition, about protecting what I have, and it's draining."

It became clear that the comfort and security David had sought were illusions. The things he had bought, instead of bringing him peace, had become chains that tied him down. His life revolved around his possessions, and the more he acquired, the less freedom he felt. The golden castle he had built was now his prison, a constant reminder of the high price of his pursuit of comfort.

David realized that his obsession with buying things, with surrounding himself with luxury and convenience, had led him away from what truly mattered. He had become so focused on acquiring more that he had lost sight of the simple joys of life—time with friends, new experiences, and the freedom to explore and grow without being tied to material possessions.

Determined to reclaim his life, David made a significant change. He began to let go of the things that no longer served him, selling off the items that demanded too much of his time and energy. He downsized his home, choosing a simpler place that required less upkeep and allowed him to focus on the things that brought him real happiness. He stopped chasing after the latest trends and started investing in experiences—travelling, learning, and spending time with the people who mattered most.

As David dismantled his golden castle, he found a new sense of freedom. Without the constant need to protect and maintain his possessions, he was able to live more fully and enjoy life without the weight of material burdens. He discovered that true comfort and security come not from the things we own, but from the freedom to live authentically, to pursue what brings us joy, and to connect with others in meaningful ways.

David's journey is a powerful reminder that while it's natural to want comfort and security, we must be careful not to let the things we own end up owning us.

The pursuit of material comfort can easily become a trap, limiting our freedom and stifling our ability to live fully. True happiness lies not in the accumulation of things, but in the experiences, connections, and freedom that allow us to live life on our own terms.

The pursuit of comfort and security can lead to the creation of metaphorical golden castles—environments designed to keep us safe and comfortable. However, these very structures can become prisons, limiting our freedom and potential. It's important to strike a balance between safety and adventure, ensuring that the pursuit of security does not hinder your ability to explore, grow, and live fully.

Chapter 7.3

Minimalism - Less Is More

I come from a culture and country where, after finishing a meal, we would crumple leftover aluminum foil into a small ball and use our fingers to play miniature soccer with it. We didn't have much growing up. We were never hungry, but on Maslow's pyramid of needs, we were at the very bottom. When you come from a culture where you never throw anything away because it might be worth something, and then move to a Western culture where you have access to everything and even valuable things don't interest you, it's a major change.

I've seen this happening on a smaller scale, but the true extent of this perspective hit me when I visited a friend's parents. I opened the door and couldn't find a place to sit; the house was full of things that had been put there and never used. My friend's parents had immigrated from West Africa, not far from where I immigrated from, so I understood their culture and perspective.

However, holding on to things or continuously seeking new things in a culture where you have access to everything can lead to having way more than you need. In one of my books, "The Camino Within," I talked about a saying my grandpa used to repeat, common in the village where I grew up: "The more you own, the more you are owned." The problem isn't getting new things; it's getting attached to them.

In my book, I discuss the impact of carrying one small thing over long distances and periods of time. I use the example of carrying an extra towel. It's easy to carry an extra towel if you're biking from home to work on a Monday morning, but not if you're carrying it across 900 kilometers of hills, valleys, and mountains in northern Spain. It's not about the weight of the object; it's about how long you're carrying it. In some of my classes, I use the example of holding a pen in my hand for 10 minutes and then asking my students how it would feel if I held it for hours. Things get heavier the longer we carry them, and this is why I believe minimalism is crucial.

As having minimalism has positively impacted my life in ways I can't imagine, I want to share with you some benefits and best practices I try to follow.

Embracing Minimalism

Minimalism is about reducing physical possessions to focus on what truly matters. It's a philosophy that encourages intentional living, financial freedom, mental clarity, and environmental responsibility.

Declutter for Clarity

Minimalism encourages reducing physical possessions to create space for what truly matters. By decluttering, individuals can focus more on experiences and relationships rather than material goods.

Intentional Living

Minimalism promotes a lifestyle of intentionality where people make conscious choices about what they allow into their lives, whether it's possessions, relationships, or activities. This helps in maintaining focus on personal values and priorities.

Financial Freedom

By purchasing less, individuals can reduce debt and save more, leading to financial stability and freedom.

This allows them to invest time and resources into things they are passionate about, rather than being burdened by unnecessary expenses.

Mental and Emotional Benefits

Minimalism can lead to reduced stress and anxiety. Owning fewer items means less maintenance and worry, leading to a more peaceful and fulfilling life. A decluttered environment also promotes mental clarity and better focus.

Personal Growth

Embracing minimalism can lead to greater self-awareness and personal growth. It challenges individuals to examine their values, priorities, and the purpose behind their actions and possessions. This self-reflection fosters personal development.

Community and Connection

Minimalism often fosters a sense of community and connection. Sharing resources and focusing on relationships rather than consumerism can build stronger, more meaningful bonds with others.

Redefining Success

Minimalism encourages redefining success beyond material wealth and possessions. Success is seen in terms of happiness, fulfillment, and the quality of one's relationships and experiences, rather than just financial achievements.

Implementing Minimalism in Your Life

Here are some practical steps to start living a more minimalistic life:

1. **Assess Your Belongings:** Take stock of what you own and identify items that no longer serve a purpose or bring joy. Gradually reduce your possessions to keep only what is essential and meaningful.

2. **Set Clear Goals:** Define what minimalism means to you and set clear goals. This could be financial savings, a more organized home, or simply reducing stress.

3. **Practice Mindful Consumption:** Before making a purchase, ask yourself if it's truly necessary and how it will add value to your life. Avoid impulse buying and focus on quality over quantity.

4. **Create a Decluttering Routine:** Regularly declutter your space to maintain a minimalistic environment. This could be a monthly or seasonal activity where you reassess your possessions and let go of excess.

5. **Focus on Experiences:** Prioritize experiences over material possessions. Invest in activities that bring joy and fulfillment, such as travel, hobbies, and spending time with loved ones.

6. **Limit Digital Clutter:** Minimalism also applies to your digital life. Organize your digital files, unsubscribe from unnecessary emails, and limit time spent on social media.

7. **Simplify Your Schedule:** Reduce commitments and obligations that don't align with your values or bring you joy. Focus on activities that

contribute to your well-being and personal growth.

8. **Practice Gratitude:** Cultivate an attitude of gratitude for what you have. This helps in appreciating the present moment and reducing the desire for more.

We Make Mistakes, Mistakes Make Us

" Poem

"Mistakes we make"– by Tarek Riman

Mistakes do not define our core,
They're just the lessons life has in store,
Each stumble, each slip, each fall we take,
Is a step forward that we must make.

Mistakes don't change who you are, or how,
They're simply markers on your way,
To guide you, shape you, make you sway.

For in each error lies a chance,
To learn, to grow, to take a stance,
Mistakes are teachers, wise and stern,
They help us see, they make us learn.

And in my life, I've known this too,
Mistakes have been my constant view,
From missed deadlines to choices wrong,
They've written in me a deeper song.

I once thought errors were my bane,
But now I see, they were my gain,
They've taught me patience, brought me grace,
And led me to this stronger place.

We build our lives, brick by brick,
But often times, the mortar's thick,
With errors, flaws, and things unplanned,
Yet here we stand, our feet in sand.

For we make mistakes, and they make us,

We Make Mistakes, Mistakes Make Us

They're not to fear, but to discuss,
Each one a step, a turn, a bend,
That helps us grow, that helps us mend.

So let your errors guide your way,
Embrace them fully, day by day,
They do not break you, they make you whole,
They carve your spirit, shape your soul.

In the end, it's not perfection we seek,
But the courage to rise, to learn, to speak,
To own our flaws, to face our fears,
And find our strength through all the years.

Mistakes make us who we are today,
They pave our path, they light our way,
So be brave, embrace the fall,
For it's in each stumble, we stand tall.

Chapter 8
Mistakes

Summary:

These chapters emphasize that mistakes are a natural and essential part of growth and do not define your character. I share the story of Mark, a bright student who initially feared that mistakes reflected poorly on him. Through encouragement, he learned to view mistakes as opportunities for learning rather than as failures. In my own journey, I've experienced how mistakes, though painful at times, have been crucial in shaping who I am today. The key takeaway is that mistakes should be embraced as stepping stones toward personal and professional growth, rather than seen as setbacks.

My Mistake: Misunderstanding Mistakes.

Chapter 8.1

Mistakes Have Nothing to Do with Your Character

Mistakes are an inevitable part of life and learning. They do not define your character but rather reflect moments of growth and experimentation. Making mistakes does not make you a bad person; it simply means you are human. It's crucial to separate your self-worth from your errors and view mistakes as valuable learning opportunities.

I once had a student named Mark who was incredibly bright and full of potential. From the first day of class, it was clear that Mark was driven by a deep desire to succeed. He was always prepared, always eager to participate, and his work was meticulous. But there was something else I noticed about him—an underlying fear of making mistakes. It was as if he believed that any misstep would be a reflection of his character, a sign that he wasn't as capable as he wanted to be.

As the semester went on, Mark continued to excel, but I could see the pressure he was putting on himself. He would often stay after class to ask for clarification on assignments, not because he didn't understand the material, but because he wanted to be absolutely sure he didn't make a mistake. It was clear that he equated his worth with his ability to perform perfectly, and the thought of making an error weighed heavily on him.

Then came the midterm exam. Mark, as expected, had studied thoroughly, but during the exam, something went wrong. He misread one of the key questions, and by the time he realized his mistake, it was too late to correct it. When the exams were graded, Mark's score was lower than he had expected, and it was clear that he was devastated.

After class that day, Mark stayed behind, visibly upset. He kept saying, "I should have done better," and "I can't believe I made such a stupid mistake." It was as if that one error had shattered his confidence, and he couldn't see past it.

I could see that Mark was equating his mistake with his self-worth, so I decided to share something with him that I had learned over the years. I said, "Mark, mistakes have nothing to do with your character. They're just a part of learning."

He looked at me, surprised. I continued, "Making a mistake doesn't mean you're not smart or capable. It just means you're human. Mistakes are opportunities to grow, to understand where you went wrong, and to do better next time. They're not a reflection of who you are as a person."

It took a moment for my words to sink in, but I could see the tension in Mark's shoulders begin to ease. We talked more about how mistakes are an inevitable part of life and learning, and how they don't define our character, but rather show that we're willing to take risks and try new things.

Over the rest of the semester, I noticed a change in Mark. He began to take more risks in his work, to challenge himself in ways he hadn't before. He still cared deeply about doing well, but he no longer let the fear of making mistakes hold him back. When he did make errors, he was able to see them for what they were—opportunities to learn, not reflections of his worth.

By the end of the course, Mark had grown not just academically, but personally as well. He had learned that his character wasn't defined by his ability to avoid mistakes, but by his willingness to learn from them and keep moving forward. It was a lesson that would serve him well beyond the classroom.

Mark's experience is a reminder that mistakes are a natural part of the learning process. They don't define who we are; they simply show that we're trying, that we're pushing ourselves, and that we're human. The true measure of our character isn't in how few mistakes we make, but in how we respond to them—whether we choose to let them hold us back or use them as stepping stones to grow and improve.

So whenever you find yourself dwelling on a mistake, remember Mark's story. Mistakes have nothing to do with your character. They are simply a part of the journey, and every error is an opportunity to learn, to grow, and to become a stronger, more resilient person.

Chapter 8.2

We Make Mistakes, and Mistakes Make Us

As I sit down to write this final chapter, I can't help but reflect on the journey that has led me to this moment. It's a journey filled with achievements, yes, but also one marked by mistakes—some small, some life-altering. And yet, it is those very mistakes that have shaped me, molded me into the person I am today. They've taught me lessons that no success could ever have imparted, and it's through them that I've found the true essence of growth and transformation.

I think back to a time in my early career, when I was still figuring out who I was and what I wanted to achieve. I was driven by the need to prove myself, always striving for perfection, always afraid of slipping up. Mistakes, I believed, were signs of failure—blemishes on the otherwise smooth surface of a successful life. I saw them as obstacles to be avoided at all costs, and I spent countless hours trying to ensure that I didn't make any.

But, of course, life doesn't work that way. No matter how careful we are, no matter how much we plan, mistakes are inevitable. They're part of being human, part of living a life that is full and real. My first significant mistake came at a time when I was juggling multiple responsibilities—my work, my personal life, my writing. I was stretched thin, trying to do everything perfectly, and in the process, I overlooked something important. I missed a crucial deadline for a project that I had been working on for months.

That moment of failure became a turning point in my life. I began to understand that mistakes are not barriers to success; they are the building blocks of growth. They force us to confront our weaknesses, to rethink our strategies, to become more resilient and resourceful. The lessons I learned from that experience were invaluable. I became more organized, more focused, and more aware of my limitations. I learned to ask for help when I needed it, to delegate when necessary, and to prioritize what truly mattered.

But the most important lesson I learned was that mistakes are not a reflection of our character—they are a reflection of our journey. They show that we are trying, that we are pushing ourselves beyond our comfort zones, that we are daring to dream and to act on those dreams. Each mistake is a testament to our courage to grow, to evolve, to become something more than we were before.

Over the years, I've made many more mistakes, both big and small. Some have been painful, others embarrassing, but each one has been a stepping stone on the path to becoming who I am today. They've taught me humility, patience, and the importance of perseverance. They've shown me that success isn't about never failing—it's about rising each time you do, armed with the knowledge and wisdom that only a mistake can provide.

I think about the people I've met, the students I've taught, the colleagues I've worked with, and the countless stories of success and failure that have crossed my path. The common thread that ties all these stories together is this: those who achieve greatness are not those who never make mistakes, but those who learn from them, who allow their mistakes to shape them, to guide them, and to make them stronger.

As I conclude this book, I want to leave you with this thought: we make mistakes, and mistakes make us. They are not to be feared or avoided but embraced as an integral part of our journey. Each mistake is a gift, a chance to grow, to learn, and to become a better version of ourselves.

So, as you move forward in your own life, remember that your mistakes do not define you. What defines you is how you respond to them—whether you let them break you or build you. Embrace your mistakes, reflect on them, and use them as the foundation for your future successes. For it is through our mistakes that we find our true strength, our resilience, and our capacity for greatness.

In the end, it's not the absence of mistakes that leads to fulfillment and success; it's the courage to face them, learn from them, and keep moving forward, knowing that each step, no matter how imperfect, is a step in the right direction.

Be brave. The credit belongs to you. The day belongs to you. The world is yours.

I will leave you with this.

"Life unbound" – by Tarek Riman

Step into the arena, facing the dust, sweat, and pain—
Take the fall, yet stand again, undeterred by the strain;
Lift your chin when others point to where you've failed,
Keep moving forward, learning, and refusing to be derailed;

Press on with all your strength toward the promise of a new day,
Chase your dreams with courage that never fades away;
Embrace your fears, and see mistakes as part of growth,
Silence the doubts of those who hesitate and never bet on both;

When the road is tough, and your steps feel heavy and slow,
When challenges arise and life's trials begin to show,
Pause if you must, but never cease,
Keep striving, keep believing, and find your inner peace;

Face both success and setback with the same steady mind,
Persist, knowing there's wisdom in each grind;
Give your all, even when it feels like it's not enough,
Discover in every obstacle a way to rise, a way to grow tough—

Stand tall, don't let your spirit dim in the night,
Rise with purpose, embrace your light,
Shape your destiny with every stride,
The architect of your journey, with nothing to hide.
Yours will be the path where true fulfillment is found,
And—above all—you'll live life unbound.

About the Author

Tarek Riman is the CEO/President of Riman Agency, a seasoned marketing expert, and a prolific author. He has taught marketing at prestigious institutions, including McGill, Concordia, York University, and JMSB. As the author of seven best-selling marketing books, including *The Camino Within*, *The SEO Way*, and *We Make Mistakes, Mistakes Make Us*, Tarek has made a significant impact in the field of marketing literature. He also serves as a board member at Yes Montreal and is the VP of Marketing and Sales at Carbon R5. Beyond his professional roles, Tarek is the founder of multiple platforms, including Riman Art, Inspiring Canadians, Montreal Tips, The UAE Blog, The Africa Blog, The Kuwait Blog, The Europe Blog, and Inspiring Arabs, where he continues to inspire and lead by example.